LIVING BEYOND RICH

~~~~~~~~~~~~~~~~~~~~~~~~~~~~~~~~~~~~

The Playbook of How to Live Your Life
Without Financial Stress, Fear, or Pain

By

Jen McDonough

PUBLISHED BY 3D PUBLISHING

Living Beyond Rich by Jen McDonough

Copyright © 2012 by Jen McDonough

Published in 2012 by 3D Publishing

Library of Congress Control Number: 2012937930

ISBN 13: 978-0984770427
ISBN: 0984770429

3D Publishing, Lindstrom, MN

CreateSpace, North Charleston, SC

What the Heck is This Book About?

Personal finance issues have become an epidemic in our society.

<u>Facts:</u>

- **7 out of 10 Americans today are living paycheck to paycheck.**

- **Money issues are the number one cause of divorce.**

- **Our world as a whole is sinking deeper into debt by the day.**

Our neighbors, family, and friends around the world are living with pain, fear, and stress over money issues. We once were too, however, our family was able to transform our situation and turn our worst days into our best days.

Our story has gained world-wide media attention and it is one that we love to share. It has given countless people just like YOU hope and inspiration.

Is this book ONLY for people that are already good at keeping track of personal finances?

NO!

Living Beyond *Rich* is for the everyday person next door who thinks winning the lottery is the only way they can become rich. It's for the person who:

- **Is just plain worn out when it comes to dealing with their finances.**

- Struggles with separating their self worth from their negative net worth and/or;

- Doesn't think they can do a budget.

I am an ordinary person who can show you how to live an extraordinary life when it comes to gaining control over your personal finances.

I am not a financial advisor, financial planner, or certified public accountant. **Despite this, my family has managed to pay off over $150,000 worth of consumer debt and an additional $30,000 in medical related expenses in just three years!**

Without any get-rich-quick schemes involved, how did we accomplish this? Were we already millionaires and just wrote out a check one day to wipe our worries away? Absolutely not.

Living Beyond Rich **will show you how from the vantage point of an ordinary American family. Similar to what families face today, our struggles were frequent throughout our journey. Some of our detours to the road to freedom included:**

- Experiencing an emotional job loss in a downturned economy.

- Having an unexpected addition to our family.

- Fighting our way through quite a few medical issues.

Question:

Who doesn't dream of becoming rich, especially in our fast moving society today where quick results are expected?

For many years, we too wanted to become RICH. We thought our financial woes would vanish if/when some money windfall would come our way.

Our dreams for becoming rich disappeared overnight when we received the news that one of our children developed a chronic lifetime medical condition. Rather than wanting to become rich, we just wanted to survive.

In needing to face our financial situation due to the large amount of medical bills coming our way, we would become gripped with terror to discover what our financial situation really looked like. **We were stunned to find ourselves DROWNING in over $150,000 of consumer debt (this did not include our first mortgage).**

We asked ourselves:

- Why was this happening to us and how had we gotten to this low point?

- Were we the only ones with financial troubles?

- How on earth were we ever going to get back on our feet again?

Have You Ever Asked Yourself Similar Questions?

Even though personal finance is a taboo subject to discuss on a personal level (the topic of people's love lives is discussed frequently while the subject of personal finances is considered too risqué to discuss), we are passionate about sharing our story.

Why?

Living Beyond Rich will change people's lives.

It is our family's playbook of how we transformed our lives. We once lived a life crammed with embarrassment, fear, shame and isolation. Today, we live a life overflowing with abundant joy, hope, freedom, peace, and empowerment. We want that same freedom and joy for you too!

Living Beyond Rich will:

- Give readers the background of what living in financial despair can do to a family.

- Provide knowledge and actionable tools to help eliminate debt.

- Share resources to learn more and achieve extraordinary success.

If you are one of the millions of people looking to transform your lives, I applaud you for taking the first steps to success by reading *Living Beyond Rich*!

I would love to have you join our movement towards gaining a rich life and look forward to connecting with you.

Live Beyond Rich!

Live Beyond Awesome!

Jen McDonough, "The Iron Jen"

Motivational Storyteller

Author, *Living Beyond Rich* and *Living Beyond Awesome*

Coach

- **Website:** http://www.TheIronJen.com

- **Twitter:** @TheIronJen

"If I can do it, YOU can do it."

Living Beyond Rich is the AWESOME playbook of one family who took their darkest days and turned them into their best days. It is real and relevant. This book demonstrates that with intentional focus and intentional action, the impossible IS possible for all of us. Let *Living Beyond Rich* take you to the extreme riches in your own life.

~ Chris LoCurto, Vice President & Speaker at Dave Ramsey's
Organization
http://ChrisLoCurto.com/

I urge you to do something special for others and yourself — read *Living Beyond Rich*. If you're sick and tired of being sick and tired, you'll be encouraged that a new life can begin today.

~Dan Miller, creative thinker at 48Days.net and author of *48 Days to the Work You Love*
http://www.48days.com
http://www.48days.net

What a way to tell us, "It is POSSIBLE!" **Learn from this family's story of getting out of the financial rat race.** Victory truly comes from within!

~ **Dr. Pei K. Boggess, Endodontist, Powerful Living Coach**
http://www.powerfulliving.tv/

~~~~~~~~~

As a physician, I see patients who are constantly grappling with trying to balance the health care needs of their family and the expenses that this incurs. *"Living Beyond Rich"* **is a must read for anyone in this situation.** It is real. It is practical and can be implemented into anyone's daily life. **A must read book.**

~ Uma S. Valeti, M.D.

~~~~~~~~~

Incredible story of triumph; doesn't get any more real than that! **Jen really captures the lows of their financial struggles, emotional battles, and though many of us are caught up in the same scenario of living paycheck to paycheck this story gives us hope that we can achieve victory.** Get ready to be inspired into taking action and move your life to truly building wealth and finally live beyond rich!

~ **Rob Clinton, Founder, 180 Career Coaching** http://www.180coach.com

~~~~~~~~~

Having had the opportunity to work as a healthcare executive for the past 32 years **I've learned that, despite our "best planning", despite having health insurance coverage, despite doing all the "right things",** unexpected health issues can create financial chaos for any family. Jen's family faced just such a situation and, in fact it was the catalyst that led them to change their spending habits. *Living Beyond Rich* will not only touch your heart but will also inspire and give hope to those struggling today. Jen's story tells us how devastating news can in fact become a blessing in disguise!

~David D. Rothschiller, Former Executive Director, St Paul Heart Clinic

Ever read a book that pulls you in instantly? This is one of those books! **It's a story of hope and transformation that stemmed from one's family financial and emotional struggles.** This book is as authentic and genuine as it gets, and it will inspire anyone who is facing financial hardships or personal challenges.

~ Kent Julian, Speaker. Author. "Not Your Normal" Life & Career Coach
http://www.liveitforward.com & http://kentjulian.com

A heart touching story of an ordinary family's transformation from living paycheck to paycheck to living beyond rich. **The inserts of wisdom and advice throughout the book will speak to the lives of those who are struggling with finances.** I trust that God will use this book to change the lives of many families and set them free from financial bondage.

~ John M. Donnelly & Associates
http://www.JohnDonnellyandAssociates.com

~~~~~~~~

This is a heartwarming story of a family's struggle with life's surprises as they walk through a new understanding of their finances and how great life can. **Beautifully written with humor and heartfelt expression.** A must read for anyone walking through life's journeys.

~ Rachel Zickefoose, Total Fusion Ministries
http://www.totalfusionministries.org/

~~~~~~~~

Real. Relevant. Inspirational. As one poor choice after another stacked itself against Jen's family, she and her husband reached a tipping point where something dramatic needed to happen; and happen quickly. **Living Beyond Rich not only tells the story of their financial transformation, it is a step-by-step guide that you can put to work immediately.**

~ Joel Boggess, author - Passion: 4 places you forgot to look
http://www.powerfulliving.tv/

~~~~~~~~

Living Beyond Rich gives inspiration to those struggling financially. **Jen and her family share their financial playbook showing that anyone can live an extraordinary life when we take action and practice personal accountability.** *Living Beyond Rich* will give you hope while helping you discover resources to become successful in life.

~ John G. Miller, Author of QBQ!, Flipping the Switch, Outstanding!, and Parenting the QBQ Way
http://www.QBQ.com

Dedicated to

my favorite husband Bob. . .my rock through storms and my best friend in life.

I love you!

Jen

"Don't Quet™" (Don't Quit)

~ Maggie McDonough

To my family, friends and readers:

Life is not a straight path; rather it is a curvy journey. When life tries to knock you down, keep moving forward. Don't sweat the small stuff and remember your goals can always shift as unexpected life events come your way. It is the intentional incremental steps we do each day that will win the race.

Don't Quet *(don't quit)!*

~ Jen McDonough "The Iron Jen"

Contents

PART FOUR
Keys to Living Beyond Rich

PART FIVE
Awesome Expert Advice

PART SIX
Awesome Resources

Awesome Foreword

As a career and life coach, I have seen people make dramatic strides forward in areas of their lives they decide are important. The motivation for making the necessary plans of action typically come from some sort of pain – job loss, business failure, relationship stress, or health challenge. How I wish people would learn to take action before the desperation of circumstances forces them to make the changes that often lead to more success.

Here's a book that gives you a clear plan in one family's story of moving to higher levels of success in their relationships, their health and their finances. *Living Beyond Rich* is packed with the wisdom and passion of deciding to get out of debt and then finding the process to involve more than just finances. Jen's determination ignited the whole family into believing that big goals are worth the effort – even if the process is not an overnight fix. Follow her example and you too will be inspired that by taking action and small consistent steps you can eat the elephant in the room (overwhelming debt).

Jen describes how management of our finances is really a reflection of our values. We are reminded of simple lessons like:

- Little consistent actions lead to big results.

- If you fill your mind with the principles of wealth and *expect* it to show up, amazing things happen.

- Live your life based on priorities – not circumstances.

- Success or failure in one area of our lives inevitably bleeds over into other areas.

- In her engaging style, Jen shows how to live an intentional financial life, how to *decide* to be a success, and then how to experience true success in multiple areas of your life.

Her family's testimony can be yours: "Our world — one that was once filled with feelings of embarrassment, shame, fear, panic, and isolation has been replaced by one complete with empowerment, peace, joy, gratitude, and freedom."

I urge you to do something special for others and yourself — read *Living Beyond Rich*. If you're sick and tired of being sick and tired, you'll be encouraged that a new life can begin today.

Dan Miller, creative thinker at 48Days.net and author of
48 Days to the Work You Love
http://www.48days.com
http://www.48days.net

PART I
A Snapshot of Our Story

JEN'S GEMZ

Live With HOPE!

We have always held to the hope, the belief, the conviction that there is a better life, a better world, beyond the horizon.

~ Franklin D. Roosevelt

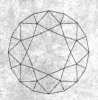

CHAPTER 1

~~~~~~~~

The Typical American Family

~~~~~~~~

Like many people today, financial ruin happened to us one dollar at a time.

Not so long ago, we were at the tipping point of financial disaster. Our financial future was dark and bleak. It would have been just a matter of time before our names would have inevitably appeared in the foreclosure section of the newspaper.

We were tired, we were broke, and we were scared.

Looking back, there wasn't any one catastrophic event that caused us to end up in this situation. At the time, however, it felt like we literally woke up one day to find ourselves swimming in debt. In fact, we weren't just swimming, we were drowning in more than $150,000 worth of debt (that did NOT include our first mortgage)!

Today, we are Living Beyond Rich. How did we do it?

Before answering that question, I have to admit that sharing our story has been one that has taken courage. Why? Because talking about personal finances is like talking about your underwear in public...it just isn't done. If you would have asked me a year ago if I would become an accomplished author and speaker, I would have thought you had the wrong Jen McDonough.

Before we started sharing our story, we were for the most part, a very private family. When it came to sharing our private lives with people outside of our family and friends, forget it. When neighbors drove by we would smile and give the 'Ms. America wave', however we would have most likely headed for the hills if one would have actually stopped to chit chat.

Fast forward to today and our personal finance story (the most personal subject in our society) has been shared worldwide. Why would our family publicly share something that is definitely an off-limits type of subject?

Simple...our story gives hope and inspiration to countless people who are experiencing the same pain we once did. We humbly share our story with audiences as an example of how people can go from being on the brinks of financial despair to living an awesome life filled with abundance, joy, and riches.

This is not a get-rich-quick money book...it is my family's story and playbook that will give knowledge and encouragement to those who are sick and tired of being broke, and for those who have had life knock them into the depths of financial despair, and/or for those who seek financial freedom.

Our road to learning how to Living Beyond Rich would begin during the worst time in our lives. It was during these painful times that we would gain skills and learn lessons that would set us up for triumph in order to Live Beyond Rich.

How would we have described our family before our life was torn apart?

We were the typical, average American family living the American dream; we had two cars, a home, and three kids.

While neither my husband nor I have college degrees, we did fairly well. I was employed as a secretary and he worked as a customer service representative. Our employers provided health insurance and our combined income seemed sufficient to support our immediate wants and needs.

> **JENSPIRATION**
>
> *Emergencies never come at a good time. Meet them head on by getting your finances in order.*

Most of our friends seemed to live similar lifestyles as we did — not poor and certainly not rich. We were just "normal." Average at best. You know, blue collar, middle class, hardworking, honest, and God-fearing.

How did we define average? Having our needs met, but not living extravagantly.

While each of us has a different view of what average living entails, scores of Americans would likely agree that the basics would include: a place to call home, a car or two, at least one or two televisions, a gaming system, cable TV, a stockpile of clothes, cell phones, and toys for all ages. Some may even include boats, motorcycles, and places to store all our treasured "stuff" to that which constitutes average.

Even though America's poor are wealthy compared to most third world countries, we do not consider clean water and a roof over our heads as "luxury items." If you were to ask most Americans today to define their standard of living, extravagant probably wouldn't be a commonly used descriptor. Most of us don't run with the truly rich and famous and we really don't expect or want to.

In our minds, extravagant living meant yachts, New York penthouses, and Beverly Hills mansions complete with servants to wait on our every need. It meant caviar at baby showers and guaranteed admission to one of the top three Universities with six (or more) figure jobs waiting once schooling was complete.

Dreaming about living extravagantly filled many of our hours over the years. Winning the lottery, receiving a significant promotion at work, and receiving an inheritance from that long lost relative were fun to dream about.

It is ironic looking back: we spent more time dreaming about changing our financial situation over the years than we actually did working on it. We always figured there would be time to work on our finances "some day." Mentally, we kept living in the "next year" frame of mind. You know... next year we will make it. Next year we will win the lottery. Next year this, next year that.

Next year never happened because we weren't living wholly in the current year.

We figured that finding our pot of gold at the end of the rainbow was our only hope for becoming rich. We certainly weren't going to find it any other way. We were just middle class and everyone knows that people can't get ahead in this world unless they're born into money or happen upon some genius invention — the "million dollar idea."

> ## JENSPIRATION
>
> *While reality isn't easy to face at times, seeing the overall picture is essential to mapping a journey to success.*

In our dreams, we drafted a plan for what we were going to do "if" our windfall came in. We spent hours and hours talking about how we'd spend our good fortune. We would quit our jobs, become entrepreneurs and do what we were passionate about. We'd travel all around the world with our kids, help some organizations, and write out a check when it came time for college.

In addition, we'd eliminate all our bills and help our extended family with their bills by "wiping the slate clean." If we only could start with a clean slate, our worries would go away, right? We'd FINALLY get to live the way we wanted to. What a life we'd have when that rainbow unexpectedly appeared and the mischievous little leprechaun came dancing onto our doorstep with the pot of gold inscribed with our names.

How many people today are dreaming of the same thing? If ONLY we could catch a break and have something good happen, THEN life would be FINALLY great we reasoned.

We had certainly heard of the lottery winners, pro athletes, and the rich and famous squandering their riches away, however, that wasn't going to be us because we had already planned how to SPEND it in advance. All we needed was the chance to make it happen. We would never be so dumb as to waste it like other people — just look at our high credit score — that alone could prove we were smart with money right?

> **JENSPIRATION**
>
> *Cash is savvy! Zero percent interest rate loans are for the naive. Debt is ALWAYS Debt.*

Like any sane person, the thought of drowning in debt never came to mind.

Maxed out credit cards, a house with an underwater mortgage, groceries bought on credit cards, and cars we couldn't afford to maintain because of high payments never entered our fairytale dreams.

Quite honestly, it doesn't sound like something anyone would have dreamed of, does it? Sadly, however, it is the road that many of us travel.

Like we once were, an astounding number of Americans are currently living paycheck to paycheck and I don't think a single one of us wished it to be this way. Heck, most of us never anticipated the pain that comes along with being in debt and quite frankly it feels unfair when it finally smacks us right upside the head. Who did this to me (us) and who do we blame? Why did this happen to us? I only bought a few things that we "needed" — how could it add up so quickly?

It must be the government's fault for taxing us so much. It must be the ever-rising costs of living. It must be the fault of my employer — they don't pay me enough; I am worth so much more. It must be the fault of those greedy credit card companies with their rising interest rates and ludicrous fees. Better yet, it's all of them — they're in cahoots to break us financially.

Not so long ago, our family asked, "Whose fault is it that we ended up living the way we did?" One minute it felt like we were living the American dream and the next, the rug was pulled out from under us. "Why did this happen to us?"

JENSPIRATION

Blaming outside persons and/or factors is always easier than looking in the mirror to see someone and/or something we don't want to see.

When it came to our lack of money, we wanted to blame someone or something and the finger of blame was always pointing elsewhere.

~~~~~~

QUESTIONS TO PONDER:

Have you ever had those types of blaming moments in your life?

Do you ever wonder why there never seems to be enough money?

Do you constantly vent about always being broke?

~~~~~~

JEN'S GEMZ

Live With Conviction — BELIEVE!

We are what we believe we are.

~ C.S. Lewis

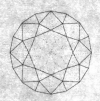

CHAPTER 2

How Does Debt Begin?

Myth: By sending my kids off to college with a credit card, it teaches them to be responsible with money.

Fact: Lenders are more than willing to teach our kids how to accumulate debt.

Stat: Only 32% of 18-year-olds understand how credit card interest and fees work.
~ Charles Schwab's 2011 Teens & Money Survey

Being in the throes of emotional turmoil causes tunnel vision that only allows us to see the immediate problems we are facing. It isn't until we are able to emotionally take a step away from the situation that we are able to see the big picture.

It wasn't until we were well along on our financial freedom journey that we could look back and discover how my family arrived at being tens of thousands of dollars in debt.

So what does it look like for someone to grow up in an ordinary upbringing only to end up in financial chaos when they have a family of their own?

In all honesty, we admit that my husband and I lacked for nothing and had very happy childhoods.

How Were We Raised?

Bob and I grew up in average American middle class families in St. Paul, Minnesota. I came from a family with three older brothers and Bob came from a family of two sisters and three brothers. We grew up in an environment where, despite our mothers having side jobs, they assumed primary responsibility for running the household and caring for the children while our fathers worked full-time.

Our parents would have told you that they often struggled to make ends meet but as kids we never felt anything but security and love.

Vacations consisted of two-to-three-hour family drives to exotic places like Duluth, Minnesota, or outdoor camping at places like Cross Lake Minnesota State Park. All of us kids would be scrunched hip to hip in our "assigned" seats (without seat belts) in our well-worn station wagon cars. We played the license plate game, sang, and had the occasional sibling disagreement. Food stops meant pulling over and feasting on the PB&J or bologna & cheese "sammiches" out of the cooler that mom packed.

Our clothes consisted of Hanes t-shirts and well worn comfortable jeans. Our homes were located in average inner city neighborhoods where moms summoned their children home for dinner by standing outside and yelling their names. "Jenny. Jennifer. Jeh-ehn-ee — dinner time!" I couldn't run home fast enough. We didn't have our own bedrooms or bathrooms but each of us had our own place at the table.

Neither of us remembers our parents using credit cards or having creditors call our house. Having mom or dad openly

discuss their finances with us kids would have been like discussing their sex lives – it just wasn't done.

Memories of our dads occasionally cracking open their wallets to give us a buck a few times a year were treasured treats. Trips to fast food places were unheard of and, until Atari came around, video games were only found at the local roller-skating rinks.

Bob and I met when I turned 20 years old. Within a month of dating, we quietly became engaged. At ages 21 and 27 we were married in a church-style wedding. We were proud to use the $5,000 generous gift of money from my parents to fund our whole wedding and honeymoon cruise trip. The wedding was complete with candy bouquets in lieu of flowers and 300+ guests that consisted of friends and family that loved to laugh. It was the "funnest" wedding I have ever attended and I don't believe I have ever danced so much in my life!

Bob and I bought our first home for $52,500 shortly before we were married in 1991. Our monthly payment was right around $500 and with our $10–$12 an hour jobs we were barely scrimping by. Ramen noodles and Mac & Cheese were our main dinner choices. It didn't matter though because we were having a blast. Our house was furnished with garage sale furniture, endless laughter, and true love.

After the first year of marriage, we started to let loose on the reigns a little.

How Debt Can Start Off Small and Grow

Throughout the next 7 years of marriage, we were considered a fun, loving couple who enjoyed having people over for cookouts, hanging out with family, and running out for occasional spontaneous purchases while not worrying about finances.

We figured what the heck, we didn't live extravagantly so we might as well treat ourselves here and there with some unexpected purchases on occasion.

As an example of our spontaneous times, we went out looking for Halloween outfits and came back with a large grandfather clock for our tiny living room. I remember another time we went out to look for a small two person cafe table and chair set. We got auction fever and ended up coming home with a 12 chair cherry wood dining room set that was as large as our dining room. Even though we wanted a 2 person table, we couldn't resist as we got a 12 person set for the bargain price of ONLY $500.

The table ended up to be the place we put our mail and I think we ended up eating at the table maybe three times before we sold it a few years later.

Bob spoiled me one or two times a year with jewelry pieces and I loved buying him whatever his heart desired as long as it fell within our credit card limit. Doing things on the spur of the moment meant FUN!

After our first few years of marriage, we started to take yearly trips like our friends were doing and thought nothing of going out to eat. If friends came to dinner with us, we enjoyed racing to grab the bill. We held football parties every weekend where we fed the gang. Our annual pig roasts were a hit! Hanging out with friends and family meant a lot to us those first few years.

> **JENSPIRATION**
>
> *Emotional spending will lead to emotions that you may not want when your bill arrives.*

Our pay increased each year and our spending habits unknowingly increased right along with it. More fun for us! We worked hard in our jobs and moved up on the pay scale. When the opportunity presented itself, we gladly worked overtime. When payday came, it was disappointing to see that Uncle Sam took most of the extra pay out for taxes.

Buying the Dream Home to Fit Our Family

Nearing our eighth year of marriage, we became parents to our daughter Maggie. We quickly discovered that being parents was the BEST! We went on to have Robbie and Max by the time Maggie was three. Before our third child was born, we made a snap decision to invest in a dream home located almost 50 miles from our work. We knew money would be tight, but the thought of raising our kids in the quiet country was thrilling.

We were perfectly okay with cutting out some of the extra things we did to give our family a better life.

We sold our first home without any problem but upon doing so realized that we had used much of the equity up in funding our lifestyle and updating our house.

No worries though, our bank assured us that we were excellent loan candidates. Because of our high credit score and combined $80,000 yearly income, we were pre-qualified for up to a $350,000 loan. Gasp!

We had planned to spend no more than $300,000 for a house, however, for a little more, we found our dream home for ONLY $339,000. We justified it by saying it had everything we needed and it wouldn't require much work compared to other houses we looked at. At the time, homes in the city and in the suburbs were going for the same if not more. We further justified our purchase by rationalizing that it was worth it to move further away to get more for our money. Our mortgage payments jumped from ~$500 to ~$2,500 (jeepers creepers it hurts just seeing that in writing!).

Being Responsible Parents Meant Having Reliable Transportation

After we moved out to our country home, we discovered that our old $500 junker vehicles would no longer do.

With three young children and with Bob and I each having a 90 mile round trip commute to work, we decided we NEEDED reliable transportation. This marked the beginning of buying and trading in new cars every two years. These weren't top end cars mind you, but average $14,000 to $20,000 cars that could get us decent gas mileage. Rather than looking at the overall price of the car, we focused on the monthly payments and what we could afford each month.

It Is Okay to Splurge on Necessity Items Isn't It?

While our high house payment and children helped curb our spontaneous purchases, in all honesty our spending habits didn't change as much as we felt they had. Sure we had cut out our yearly vacations and some other small items, but we still had our fair share of

JENSPIRATION

Self awareness is empowering! When we put boundaries in our life is when we have freedom.

15

unplanned and unbudgeted spontaneous fun. I remember Bob going in for an oil change and coming home with a new car (it was around the two year mark for trading in anyways he figured). How exciting was that? That was just us. Being spontaneous meant fun and fun is who we were.

Things weren't quite as carefree as they had been when we were younger, but we still managed to spend. We justified our spontaneous spending because we bought necessity items. Things like reliable *new* vehicles were a necessity...or so we thought.

The Joneses Know How to Live

Our lifestyle mirrored those around us although our lifestyle didn't seem nearly as extravagant as others in nearby neighborhoods. "Wow, look at how THOSE people lived we would think," when we drove by some of the upscale neighbors. They must be doing really well.

While we didn't give a hoot about keeping up with the Joneses, we sure did enjoy seeing how they lived. It was pleasurable to imagine what our lives would be like once we got to that point in life where everything became easy.

JENSPIRATION

Trash the credit cards and opt for cash — your future will thank you.

What Does Living Without a Spending Plan Look Like?

As far as our finances were concerned, we subscribed to the "bonus" method. We calculated it as a bonus if we saved money or didn't spend money on something. For example, we would go without a barbecue grill (and tell ourselves that we had "saved" that money) but then if friends were coming over, we'd decide that we suddenly needed one. Rather than slowly compare and shop for the best bargains, we charged out of the house with our credit card in hand ready to hunt one down.

We started at the lowest priced one and worked our way up. Comparing, searching, and shopping for the BEST one for what we had "saved" to spend. The thrill of the chase made it seem like we were on a mission. When the hunt was over, we would pat ourselves on the back for ONLY buying the $200 barbecue grill instead of the $300 upgraded version. The $100 we "saved" would be our "reward" to spend on something else — it was 'bonus' money.

If we looked at our grocery bill and saved 30% we were doing great — never mind that we bought stuff we wouldn't ordinarily buy or stuff that we already had in the cabinet (how many mustard containers can one family go through in a life-time?). We saved 30%...bonus! It was the thrill of the hunt and a victory of sorts to see "how much we could save."

> **JENSPIRATION**
>
> *Mom was right. When we did something dumb, she'd ask us, "If the other kids were jumping off the bridge would you jump too?" Normal doesn't mean it is right.*

We thought we were okay as long as we didn't take yearly vacations that we couldn't afford. In addition, our furniture was old and other than my work attire, our wardrobes came from Target and Wal-Mart.

A Family Must Be Doing Great If They ONLY have One Credit Card

Because we had ONLY one credit card we thought we were doing better than most. We considered anything under the max credit limit as "our money." We would use "our money" until we hit the max, pay it down a little and then run it back up and then repeat it again.

(Does any of this roller coaster type of living ring a bell? Great, then it means you are living like most people today.)

We loved to give gifts for the heck of it and thought nothing of dropping $30 to $50 on a little surprise or token of appreciation for friends or family.

We managed our money as if we had money trees growing in the backyard. We figured it was okay as long as we were making it, we were kind, and we gave.

> ## JENSPIRATION
>
> *Credit card and finance companies are experts at luring us in to make it feel like we are cheating them, while in reality, we are the ones being cheated.*

We were definitely the people you wanted to go to when selling raffle tickets for charity, selling those yummy Girl Scout cookies, or taking collections at work. We even managed to toss a $10 or $20 bill into the church offering each week depending upon what we had left in our wallets.

Little Habits Can Wreak Havoc

With our new house being so far away, we didn't see our family and friends as much. However, we still enjoyed getting together on the weekends to grill burgers and brats on the deck. We treasured those times. This served as our social/family entertainment. Friday and Saturday nights consisted of movie nights at home with either Chinese takeout or pizza. Sunday afternoons consisted of going out to eat at places like Olive Garden, Don Pablo's, and

Outback Steak house. The weekends were used to recharge our batteries so we'd be ready for Monday mornings.

Little did we know that we were NOT recharging our batteries, we were draining our lives because of our mindless spending.

Since Bob and I worked long and hard during our four 10-hour days each week in addition to our long commutes, we considered going out for daily $5 to $10 lunches (each) to be a necessity. We left the house at 6:00 a.m. and got home around 6:00 p.m. Marge, my saintly mom, watched our kids while we were at work and we felt very blessed. On many days we would

> **JENSPIRATION**
>
> *Financing $5 on a credit card each day for coffee is stealing $1,865 a year from one's freedom when you are in debt.*

be tired from our long days and, rather than cook, we'd pick up fast food on the way home to feed the kids.

When Our Spending Increased, Our Quality Family Time Decreased

Like many families today, we were a busy family on the go. Besides our long workdays, during hockey season our schedules consisted of rushing around between the scheduled 6:00 p.m.– 10:00 p.m. practices on school nights. Bob coached two of the kids' hockey teams so weekends meant running here and there for hockey-related events. The busier our life was, the more we frequented fast food drive-thrus. Our family's commute times became family time. Hockey rinks were used as social hours for the kids and it also gave them a chance to get some exercise.

When hockey season was done, we found other fun things to do as a family. We visited theme parks, interactive museums, music festivals, and parades. It was easy to drop $50 or more on any one outing.

As the kids got older, our running all over the place increased.

There were hardly any hours left in the day for mom and dad's social time. My social time consisted of biking once a week with my road bicycle crew and Bob played wiffle ball once a week. Our kids were learning that the busier our lives were the better. Gone were the peaceful family dinner hours where we would sit down together, give thanks for the food in front of us, and chat about the day. Chaotic schedules were our normal. Quarter Pounders and fries were the main dish and our designated seats were on four wheels.

Using Creative Money Methods Without a Budget Doesn't Work

> **JENSPIRATION**
>
> *Spending 5 minutes a day on a budget will lead to more riches than spending 2 hours a day in front of the TV.*

(For those out there that are already good at personal finances, this section is probably going to seem unimaginable. For others that fall into the over 50% of our population who don't use a budget, you will probably be able to relate to our former way of 'budgeting'.)

As far as tracking our finances, we regularly utilized the "guesstimate" method of budgeting. We would reluctantly check our bank balances about once or twice a year. In our minds, only "nerds" who didn't like to have any fun checked their accounts routinely. We on the other hand were free spirits who relied on rough estimates. Besides, if we didn't check the account, we wouldn't have to face the fact that there might not be enough there to do what we wanted. Our "rough estimates" were easy to deal with.

Moving Money Around Doesn't Make One a Financial Guru

We didn't need to worry because when we found ourselves a little short, there seemed to always be a willing lending source... including our own retirement accounts!

As far as finding ways to make our money work for us, Bob and I considered ourselves savvy EXPERTS. We knew how to move money around like financial professionals!

Every few years when our line of credit and credit card became maxed out, we would take out a 401k loan to pay our loans down. This allowed us to "free up" more of "our money." We were told (and believed) that using the 401k loans was smart because we paid ourselves back — we viewed it as free money and we saved ourselves the interest of paying that money to some bank. Experts advised us that doing this was the wise thing to do.

Our credit score hung in the upper 700's and it was proudly and boldly draped across any credit/loan application we filled out. Our high credit score gave us a status of sorts; it told us that we were good enough and deserved some sort of recognition. Heck, even the flurry of mail-based credit card offers said we had earned the right to have and use credit.

(It is kind of ironic when we look back on it. Bragging about a credit score was okay...bragging about "debt" was taboo. What is the difference? A high credit score didn't make us better with our money...it simply made us great customers for more debt.)

A Poor Person's View of Purchases

As with a majority of people today, the notion of looking at what we could afford each month versus looking at the overall cost of something was how we lived. A $300 to $400 payment here and there didn't seem like much. Zero interest rate offers on big ticket items were even better as we reasoned it would be paid off before the promotional period expired. Heck, it just seemed like a great "deal."

What we found is that these purchases were certainly "no deal" whatsoever. Financing companies make their living off of people with these kinds of attitudes.

In addition, by looking at our purchases as monthly payments versus the total cost, we were essentially living like poor people. Ouch! Why do I say this? Because it is true. In Tom Stanley's book *The Millionaire Next Door*, his statistics point out that the average millionaire doesn't look at the cost per month when buying something...they look at the overall price of what something costs. Sounds easy to understand, but how many car companies can you name that advertise the total price before they advertise the car payments? Not many.

Our poor person's perspective of purchasing things based on what we could afford in monthly payments as well as our 'creative' budgeting techniques got us into major trouble over the years.

Refinancing Is Not the Answer to Living Rich

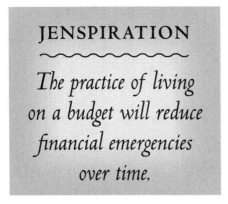

JENSPIRATION

The practice of living on a budget will reduce financial emergencies over time.

Like numerous others who ended up in a financial mess, we had refinanced our first house several times, using up the equity during a time when house values were increasing. Like most, it was assumed we could continue that practice with our current house as well. In fact, it was how we planned to finance our kids' college. Our original 30-year loan would have probably taken us over 40–50 years to pay off.

By continuing to refinance we naively assumed we were winning the money game.

Although it is easy to read in a few chapters how someone else got into to financial trouble, it is certainly difficult to see when it is your own story. After all a good number of us are trying to play the money game like everyone else. The money game as we all know it is to get more stuff right? Besides, wasn't it true that everyone bought their stuff and then paid for it later?

Is Debt Sophisticated or Just Plain Dumb?

It strikes me as strange, as we look back on those times, how we can justify our actions with our choice of words — words that mean the same can sound so different. Take for instance the words "financing" and "debt." They both mean the same, however, financing is for the sophisticated and debt is for the poor, right?

Debt is a very negative, ugly word in our society. If we had been asked several years ago if "we were in debt" we would have probably looked at you and shook our heads adamantly no, even though we were head over heels in debt. Being in debt meant one was losing a home or filing bankruptcy, right?

We weren't in debt, we were just good at financing. We knew how to juggle money.

JENSPIRATION

We live in a world of instant gratification. We graduate from school, get married, and expect to have the same standard of living as our parents, forgetting that they already worked their entire lives to achieve those standards. When we borrow our way to instant gratification, it is the lender who owns and controls our privileged lifestyle, not us.

In short, money appeared to be magical and mystical to us. There were always ways to get more money, or so we assumed. Places loved to lend us money and we became good at finding them! Banks loved us and credit card companies continuously sought us out. That is how we "found our money."

What Did All This Add Up To?

While your story may not be exactly the same, I am sure those who are not budgeting, yet struggling with finances can see some similar attitudes of how they view and use money as well.

So what did our attitudes and actions eventually end up to costing us?

Over a 17-year period, we would eventually rack up more than $150,000 worth of debt that did not include our first mortgage. Besides costing us money, it also robbed us of many sleepless nights and extreme amounts of stress, worry, and pain.

If we hadn't changed our finances when we did, I cringe to think where we would be today. The dangerous path we were on would eventually have left us financially devastated. Without realizing it we were had been living on the proverbial slippery slope and were losing our footing — fast.

QUESTIONS TO PONDER:

How were you raised and did your parents teach you how to budget?

How has this affected your life now?

In looking over your financial predicament can you see how you've arrived where you are today?

JEN'S GEMZ

Live With INTENTION!

Our intention creates our reality.

~ Wayne Dyer

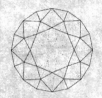

CHAPTER 3

〜〜〜〜〜〜

The Crisis That Triggered Our Financial Makeover

Myth: Everyone should instinctively know how to handle their finances.

Fact: Financial competency is a learned skill.

Stat: Only 43% of 18-year-olds know how to balance a checkbook or check the accuracy of a bank statement. ~ Charles Schwab's 2011 Teens & Money Survey

〜〜〜〜〜〜〜〜〜〜〜〜〜〜〜〜〜〜〜〜〜〜〜〜

Like most people who appear to be living the American dream on the outside, but are not in control over their personal finances, our emergencies started to become more and more frequent over the years.

When we were in the middle of a crisis, we only saw the immediate need rather than seeing the bigger picture surrounding us.

That is what it is like for many who are feeling the stress of financial burdens today. We are looking to soothe the immediate pain versus looking at the actual root cause. When the pain is gone, we usually go back to our old methods of what we know.

It is when we cannot soothe the pain away that many of us decide to either stay stuck in the muck, make an effort to try to change, or decide to take our worst days and turn them into our best days.

Our incredible journey that we share with you today stemmed from one of those painful mucky life-type moments. While it didn't feel rosy at the time we now look back and are appreciative as it transformed our lives.

Our journey began the day our world turned upside down; it was the day our 7-year-old son was diagnosed with a lifelong medical condition.

It was during this dark time in our lives that we learned the most valuable lessons that would lead us into wealth.

Now that you have the backdrop of who we were and how we lived, here is the beginning of our story that led us to Living Beyond Rich...

Once Upon A Time...Our Life Was About To Change

It was the best of times. It was the worst of times.

It was winter in the Midwest and our lives were full of happiness. Two months before our world would be turned completely upside down, I achieved a huge life goal by completing my first Ironman Triathlon (the day I became The Iron Jen). Ironman consists of a 2.4 mile swim, a 112 mile bike ride, and a 26.2 marathon, in less than 17 hours.

I had trained and planned for this monumental event for over a year. Even though life was intentionally focused on training while working full-time, my first priority was being a mom to our three awesome kids (now 9-, 7-, and 5-years-old), and a wife to my awesome husband. I was successful at juggling many responsibilities during this busy time.

Making the journey to becoming an Ironman was even more significant given that I was not a swimmer, a runner, or a pro-cyclist. In fact, I couldn't run two blocks just a few years prior. I was an ordinary person who wanted to do something extraordinary.

JENSPIRATION

We become what we believe.

During my year-long training for this one-day event, I became an expert in some important life skills including time management, discipline, and perseverance. These skills along with the strength of my faith and setting goals allowed me to work through many barriers during that incredible journey.

My priority of being mom and wife came first, so I implemented creative training methods to train with and around my
family. Killer time management skills ensured that my priorities

and perspective were kept in balance during the 12-month training journey.

Completing Ironman was one of the coolest things I have ever done outside of my commitment to family and God. Working through the tough patches including the overwhelming mental and physical fatigue made the victory of completing the Ironman even sweeter.

JENSPIRATION

Wishes are just dreams with no actions. . . GOALS are dreams with actions.

After becoming an Ironman was achieved, life settled down quite a bit. Our family life seemed blissful and full of joy.

We found time as a family to take on a new adventure in life — learning how to bake (I wasn't Betty Crocker®). We celebrated our experiments and found humor in our baking blunders. Outbursts of giggles were frequent and conversations often included "Mom, is the black crust edible?"

"Just scrape it off honey."

The chocolate chip cookies were our favorites!

Life was sweet, delicious, and satisfying.

The only glitch around this time occurred when our 7-year-old son Robbie began struggling with reading. We became more concerned when we noticed that out of the blue he started to have bed-wetting accidents. We also noticed episodes where he'd be guzzling water as if he had just walked across the desert.

Not being excessively concerned, but knowing it had to be addressed, we made an appointment with a family doctor the following week.

Other than a few bumps here and there our life had been charmed and blissful, but all that was about to change...

The Day Our World Changed

It was January 12, 2009, and a horrific snowstorm hit as they often do during Minnesota winters. Traffic was inching along at a snail's pace. After a long ten-hour workday it seemed to take forever to drive home.

Lost in thought, I was startled when my cell phone rang. I glanced at the clock and remembered that Bob was with our son Robbie at the doctor's office to address his nightly accidents. I was eager to hear what the doctor had to say.

When my husband Bob spoke, his voice sounded funny...like he was in shock or something.

JENSPIRATION

Always choose kindness. How many people around us are in the midst of their own crisis and we don't even know it? Being kind to people around us could be an unexpected soothing balm for them and us.

"Jen" he said. There was some more silence. He didn't sound like himself at all and I wondered what they had found out at the appointment. "Jen...the doctor thinks Rob has type I, diabetes."

Silence.

"Jen, the doctor thinks he has type I diabetes...we need to take him down to the emergency room right now for some tests. They want to admit him immediately."

Life as I knew it changed in an instant. I no longer noticed the snowstorm or the traffic around me. I didn't quite think I understood what Bob had just said. With a mindless nod and a brief goodbye I struggled to rush to my family. It was the longest commute of my life.

We arrived at the emergency room where they asked Robbie to put on a hospital gown. In seeing his excessively thin torso, my hand immediately flew to my mouth to cover my shocked gasp. Oh my, how and when had he gotten so skinny? His arms looked like pipe cleaners and each rib showed a clear pronounced outline. He'd always had a slight build for a 7-year-old, however, his physique seemed to have changed dramatically overnight.

> **JENSPIRATION**
>
> ~~~~~~
>
> *A mom's job description seems to include having concern for our children no matter what their age.*

I was horrified at how little and fragile he looked, sitting there in that paper-thin cotton hospital gown. He had lost so much weight. Even his eyes appeared to be sunken in. I couldn't get over how pencil thin his arms were. "What kind of mom had I been not to notice this?" I silently scolded myself.

The sight of his small frail body sitting on the narrow ER bed brought instant tears to my eyes.

Even as a newborn, Robbie was hypersensitive to physical sensations and he screamed during the blood draws. The memories of his terrified shrieks rang in my ears afterwards as we waited to find out what was actually wrong and what the next steps were.

The ER physician came in to see us a little while later. He introduced himself and asked us a few questions. "It seems Robert has type I diabetes." He explained. I looked intently at him when I asked if he was sure. As a protective mom, I wanted proof. If you couldn't prove it that meant there were other possibilities.

"Yes, he does have type I diabetes." He confidently confirmed with a nod of his head. His voice and eyes were full of empathy. "His blood sugars are 498. Normal blood sugars are under 100. The insulin producing cells in his pancreas are unable to function properly which is an indication of type I diabetes."

We would come to learn that Robbie would be receiving 5–7 shots a day. In addition, he would need to have his blood tested at least 4-6 times a day. His survival would now require insulin deliveries for the remainder of his life. Unlike the more commonly known type 2 diabetes, type I diabetes is an autoimmune condition that affects 1 out of every 300 people. Changes in diet and/or exercise habits wouldn't affect the need for outside insulin for his body to function. Suggestions from well-meaning people who offered that we consider radical new fad diets, consider gastric bypass surgery, and/or cut out sugar were not relevant.

> **JENSPIRATION**
> ~~~~~~~~
> *Recognizing the difference between true wants versus true needs is key to Living Beyond Rich.*

Feeling an undeniable pull towards finding a cure, we would turn to our faith and medical research.

Within a month of Robbie being diagnosed, I obsessively poured through over 300 medical research studies. There was an undeniable obsession to find a solution; to find him a *cure*. After contacting medical sources around the country, I learned that Robbie didn't qualify for any clinical studies in our area.

I was relentless in my search for a cure and we eventually found a medical research study being conducted outside of Denver at

> **JENSPIRATION**
> ~~~~~~~~
> *We all get moments of clarity in our lives that lead to transformation.*

the Barbara Davis Medical Center. The study consisted of 16 visits (which totaled about 48 days) over a two-year period. Our goal was to get him enrolled in the study as soon as he was eligible which would be in June on his 8th birthday (Robbie would go on to become the youngest and lightest patient in the study).

The purpose of the study was to treat his immune system so that it would temporarily quit attacking its own cells. Our hopes centered on the dream that our son would be the exception to the rule and that his cells would last until a cure was found. Once the cells were gone, they were gone.

On the day Robbie was first diagnosed, our world was turned upside down and then given a good shake just for good measure. While the memory of that day is awful, it serves as a gift as it was also the day our family began our transformation into the people we are today.

But the journey wasn't easy. The life-changing journeys never are...

QUESTIONS TO PONDER:

What pivotal life defining moments, financial or otherwise, have sprung up in your life?

What has been the outcome of these defining moments? Has it affected your life in a positive or negative way?

JEN'S GEMZ

Live With COURAGE!

All our dreams can come true, if we have the courage to pursue them.

~ Walt Disney

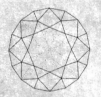

CHAPTER 4

~~~

Waking Up With an Underwater Mortgage and an Empty Bank Account... Our Freedom Journey begins

Myth: Debt is no big deal.

Fact: Debt has become an epidemic.

Stat: U.S. household 2009 debt, including mortgages was at $13.5 trillion. If we divide that among every man, woman and child in America, the average debt is $43,874 per person.
~ The Federal Reserve, March 2010

Like any tragedy, ours hit in the blink of an eye. As with anyone who has ever had a life-altering event, we would find our lives changed forever. We just never realized it would be for the better.

Until this point, we couldn't have understood what it felt like to wake up one morning feeling great only to emotionally hit rock bottom by that evening.

As a parent, having something terrible such as a chronic condition happen to your child feels like your heart is being ripped out.

Our hearts were filled with a deep raw pain and a feeling of helplessness.

Learning how to care for Robbie those first few weeks was extremely overwhelming and, at times, we felt inadequate in learning how to manage this chronic condition. There were many days we were emotionally exhausted as it involved much more than we had ever realized. As a mom, I worried about his future. Who would take care of him when he couldn't take care of himself? Whom would he marry? What would he do when he went off to college? What if there was a natural disaster and we couldn't get to his insulin for a few days?

It would have been much easier if Bob or I could have been diagnosed with this condition rather than one of our children.

Even though we knew that people all over the world were dealing with much worse in life, we still struggled a great deal with overwhelming anger, sadness, and sense of loss those first few months.

It was during this emotional time, that we would soon find ourselves financially devastated as well.

I remembered leaving the pharmacy after being discharged from the hospital. I found myself sobbing in the parking lot holding his one month supply of medicine that cost us more than $500 — it was $500 we didn't have and it might as well have been $5,000 the way it felt at the time.

Medical bills started making their way to our mailbox within the first few weeks of Robbie's hospital stay. Even though we had great insurance, we still faced thousands of dollars in out-of-pocket expenses for his medical care. And, when it rains, it pours. In addition to the annual $4,800 out-of-pocket expense we were going to incur, our car unexpectedly required a $2,000 repair.

> ### JENSPIRATION
>
> *Be intentional and set your own "Independence Day" date to start your financial transformation.*

Up until this point, we had always found ways to cover our expenses. A few months earlier, we had resorted to taking out our third 401k loan. The loan basically covered our living expenses from the months prior. Although I had a lump in my stomach when we took the loan out, we still continued to live the way we were living. We told ourselves eventually the day would come when we would take the time to "sit down and work things out"...we just weren't ready yet and figured we would deal with it at a later time. Next year, perhaps.

Well...our time had come and we now needed to figure it out. Our old methods of finding money had finally been depleted.

When we desperately started to "look" for money, we found our credit card was maxed out, our house was underwater, and our line of credit was sitting at $3,000. Bob had two 401k loans that we were paying on for another two years and my 401k loan wasn't due to be paid off for another five years.

Certainly the bank would help us we thought. They had always been so nice to us in the past. After making numerous calls and applying for several loans, we were declined. So much for our high credit score helping us out when we really needed it.

Here we were...the self proclaimed "financial experts" who could seek out the best interest rate loans on the planet and we were now knocked on our butts from this one life event.

We were stunned, shocked, and horrified to realize that our financial situation was in dire straits.

It was shear panic to discover we couldn't afford Robbie's airline tickets to Denver for the medical study. Fear ate at us as we also discovered we were unable to find a means to pay for the medical bills that were starting to roll in.

We were in no way prepared with any sort of emergency fund, and the people sending the bills did not care.

We felt financially trapped with nowhere to run to and no one to turn to. We blamed our financial woes on an expensive medical condition that devastated our lives overnight, not on our lack of preparing for the unthinkable.

We were stunned that a few thousand dollars in medical expenses could cripple us. Our paychecks seemed to be gobbled up like chum in a shark-feeding frenzy before each month was over.

> **JENSPIRATION**
>
> *Solutions come when hope and belief exist.*

It felt like we were marooned in the middle of the sea with no land in sight, no map, and a hurricane all around us.

We were frustrated, sad, scared, and in shock from the medical hurricane that touched our lives. We were also faced with the embarrassment, fear, and shame of not being able to afford the bills that were coming our way. We felt alone and hopeless.

We had some financial resources available through our employers, but we were too scared to call. Besides, we thought those resources were really more for people who were out of control with their finances due to gambling or other spending addictions. We didn't think we were out of control; we just needed to figure out how to pay for necessities.

Had anyone else felt the same way we wondered?

> ## JENSPIRATION
> ~~~~~~
> *Using credit cards to rack up some happiness here and there is a temporary pleasure that will risk your future.*

As the weeks went on, sifting through the bills that filled our mailbox became emotionally draining and increasingly frightening. Each new bill seemed to zap our energy. Who knew what bill or bad news may be lurking inside those envelopes?

Checking the mail felt like we were playing a game of Russian roulette. We had begun to get so drained from seeing the bills that we started to despise opening our mailbox. The everyday mundane activity of getting the mail now generated a negative physical reaction each time we approached it. Our stomachs would turn in knots and our muscles tensed as we opened the box. It was almost as if we were kids waiting for a monster to jump out at us.

Those particularly "scary" envelopes that held large amounts due were tossed into what we named our Pile of Denial. If we didn't open the ones in the Pile of Denial, it meant we could put off the pain of seeing what was really inside.

> ## JENSPIRATION
> ~~~~~~
> *Excuses become roadblocks in our life that prevent us from becoming the people we were meant to be.*

What the heck happened to that family that was living the American dream? The ones who appeared to have the perfect financial life from the outside?

It was as if we woke up one morning after having a bucket of ice water tossed on us. We were left shaking our heads in disbelief asking ourselves, "How did we get to this point?"

Certainly, we never thought it would happen to us. This happened to other people not "people like us." We were honest, hardworking, tax-paying people who did not live extravagantly. We had good health insurance and we lived clean lives. We were God-fearing and honest people of faith. We had many years of fun, but it was good clean fun.

Wasn't that enough? All we had to show for our hard work was a table full of bills, an underwater mortgage, and an empty bank account.

Standing in line praying our almost maxed out credit card had enough left on it to pay for our groceries was definitely not the life we envisioned when we got married 17 years prior.

Where had we gone wrong?

~~~~~~

QUESTIONS TO PONDER:

Have you ever had some life event hit you so hard that you felt your world thrown off kilter?

Have these life events provoked you to ask yourself, "Where did I go wrong?"

~~~~~~

PART II
The Beginning of Our Freedom Finance Journey

JEN'S GEMZ

Live With FAITH!

Take the first step in faith. You don't have to see the whole staircase, just take the first step.

~ Martin Luther King, Jr.

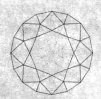

CHAPTER 5

Is There Help Out There?

Myth: Bankruptcy is an easy way out of a financial crisis.

Fact: Bankruptcy is rated as one of the most stressful life events a person can go through.

Stat: 19% of bankruptcy filers are college students. ~ USA Today

When storms hit our lives, it is easy to expect our Creator to fix things to exactly the way we want them and within our timeframes. It is as if we want to put our prayers in as a fast food restaurant order and expect it to be our way and delivered within 30 minutes or our money back. "Yes, I'll have the number four with a side of $150,000, and a piece of cake for dessert."

Who doesn't want problems in our lives fixed pronto?

It reminds me of the parable of a person who was caught in a flood. When rescuers came by to help, the person responded by saying, "Oh no thanks, I prayed and God will save me." When the second set of rescuers came by in boats, the person said the same thing, "No, I don't need your help, I have prayed to God and He will save me." Finally, when the flood had reached the rooftops, the last boat of rescuers came by and begged the person to get in the boat. "No thanks, God will save me." The person drowned. When the person arrived in heaven, the person asked, "God, I had faith YOU were going to save me, but YOU let me drown. Why did YOU let this happen?" God answered, "I did try to save you, I sent three rescue boats your way, but you refused to get in."

When our world was turned upside down our reaction was similar to the person stranded in the flood. We prayed for a fix as we were drowning, but wanted to ignore the financial rescue boats that would be sent our way because it wasn't how we pictured ourselves being saved. This is the same attitude we find in people all around us today that are struggling. They are looking to be rescued, but want to ignore the rafts that are within their reach.

What was life like right before we jumped on the raft sent our way?

It was terrifying to come to the realization that we couldn't cover our daily expenses without borrowing money, much less afford a plane ticket for our son's first trip to Denver. It would only be a matter of a few short weeks before we would start to fall behind on our bills. Once that happened, we couldn't even fathom how we were going to make it through this tragic time in our lives.

Along with all this stress, layoff talks were starting to be discussed at my place of work. The amount of stress and fear that had built up at this point was almost indescribable.

The question of "why us" played over liked a broken record.

As parents, we were heartbroken, scared, ashamed, angry, and sad.

We couldn't see beyond the day we were living when our church announced they were offering an online financial course through a person we had never heard of before. The name of the course was Financial Peace University. The host was a guy who was featured on the Fox Business News and who had a national talk radio show.

His name was Dave Ramsey.

Even though the timing seemed to eerily correlate with our financial troubles, it didn't register at first that this was a life raft being sent our way. In all honesty, we believed a financial class was meant for "THOSE" people who didn't know how to manage their money. We weren't one of "THOSE" people. Besides, the thought of taking a class to learn how to manage money was embarrassing and humbling.

Our reasons for not wanting to take responsibility for *investing* in our future mirror what scores of families are using today. Some of our excuses included:

Excuse #1: "We would, <u>but</u> we can't afford it"

Somehow, we felt we couldn't afford the course, but we could afford to eat lunch out every day. Why? Basically, it's hard to see the storm when you're standing smack dab in the middle of it.

Like the parable "teach a man to fish and he'll never go hungry again," we eventually learned that this was a chance to learn something, and it was an *investment in our future,* not a line item expense. Hindsight being 20/20, it was one of those crystal clear moments of transformational opportunity that would reshape our lives.

Excuse #2: "We would, <u>but</u> we don't have time"

Further adding to our negative attitude was the fact that we were short on time. Who has time to watch some finance courses?

We both worked full-time, we had three kids busy in sports, and had no free time in our hectic life.

JENSPIRATION

Teaching our kids by example that time invested wisely is healthier than teaching them to fill their days up with busyness.

Hindsight shows us that we, in essence, placed a higher value on keeping busy than we did on getting our life in order.

Excuse #3: "We would, <u>but</u> were not taught to as kids"

I was 16-years-old when I got my first checking account and it felt great. I was 18 when I got my first credit card and that felt cool. During our early 20s, we "collected" department store cards like they were trophies. Having credit cards seemed to be the badges of honor to validate us as *responsible* adults.

We naively assumed that the lending companies were supposed to teach us how to handle our finances. After all, weren't they more experienced than our parents? Sadly, they "taught" us that debt made us great consumers and therefore more credit worthy.

The same insecurities we faced in learning how to care for our son mirrored our belief about our finances. "We are not good at this stuff." We wanted to yell, "This is NOT us...we weren't taught this stuff as kids!"

Besides all the above excuses, we were at the end of our rope and did not believe a class would help us.

It took a few days, but we realized this raft must not be ignored although we very much wanted to. We reluctantly took money from our line of credit to pay the course fees up front. Spending money on some course that wasn't going to help us chapped our hides big time. We baulked at the $99 investment.

So...did we finally get excited after we signed up and were ready to begin?

NOPE!

We still had a huge chip on our shoulders when we started the online courses. We needed money and not some class we silently complained.

The only possible positive thing that could come out of these courses was that perhaps we would become lucky and pick up a trick or two.

Just thinking of our own childish attitudes back then has me chuckling today. Literally, it was as if we were throwing a tantrum about going through with it. If that was one of our kids acting that way about something they needed to do, I would have given them a gentle yank to the short hairs on the back of their heads as a reminder to snap out of it. I wonder if God sometimes wants to gently pull the backs of our hairs too? Just a yank here or there as a means to lovingly say, "Hey, snap out of it, you know better than that!"

The Raft Was Really a Lifesaver

Wow, how wrong had we been about "some financial class" not helping us.

The class was essentially our starting line to learning how to take ownership and control of our finances which led us down the path to learning how to live a life full of abundance.

QUESTIONS TO PONDER:

Are you ready to start your finance freedom journey or are you allowing excuses to get in your way?

Do you see any rescue rafts in your sight right now? If so, what is preventing you from hopping on board?

JEN'S GEMZ

Live With PASSION!

Every great dream begins with a dreamer. Always remember, you have within you the strength, the patience, and the passion to reach for the stars to change the world.

~ Harriet Tubman

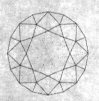

CHAPTER 6

~~~~~~~~

First Steps to Freedom

Myth: A budget is for people who only have a college degree in finance.

Fact: A budget is for the everyday person who wants to tell their money what to do versus having their money dictate their lives.

Stat: 56% of Americans do not have a budget. ~ 2010 Consumer Financial Literacy Survey

~~~~~~~~

Give me a shout if you are with me on this. Who really "yearns" to take time to work on boring finances? Seriously, who wants to be stuck in front of a computer looking at bank statements and budgets when there is so much fun going on in the world? Besides that, doesn't one need to be naturally 'gifted' with some super national finance ability in order to be good finances?

If you can relate to any of the questions above, I think you fall into the majority of what most readers would have answered as well. It certainly is where we would have fallen as well when we first started.

Since we were busy as well as short on time and patience to learn about finances, we decided that *I* would watch the finance course while Bob had the kids at hockey.

What happened?

Even with my crossed arms stance, watching the first online course was like flicking the light switch on for me. Within the first 15 minutes, my arms slowly uncrossed and my scowl faded away to a look of intense interest.

Dave Ramsey, as it turned out, is a no-nonsense, easy-to-understand finance expert and he was speaking directly — to me. And everything he said made sense. It's like he knew us...

My attitude went from being irritated about watching a nerdy online personal financial course to discovering that this could be a life-changing solution. The advice made sense and a seed was planted that changed the course of our lives...

That seed was HOPE.

Seeing people just like us talk about their struggles with finances made me realize we were not the only ones going through this. Hearing ordinary people like us talk about turning their finances around lit a small flicker of hope that we could do the same thing.

The online course touched my heart. The thought of living with peace and empowerment around finances seemed impossible, however, this class claimed it was possible.

For us, it also meant a solution to affording Robbie's travel to Denver, which meant a possible cure.

JENSPIRATION

Day one draws the line in the sand and says enough is enough. This is the starting line for Living Beyond Rich.

Talk about inspiration for motivation!

Our praying for a solution wasn't going to come as a windfall of money, like we wished for, it was going to come in the form of knowledge. Dave Ramsey was giving us a fishing pole and we were learning to cast a line rather than wait for the fish to be given to us. We had prayed for a solution and this could be it!

What did the financial program look like?

It was a series of 7 steps (information on these steps can be found at Dave Ramsey's website at http://www.daveramsey.com). The first three steps were what excited me the most as I saw it helping our most immediate needs. The steps were as follows:

1. **Starter Emergency Fund** — Save $1,000 for a starter emergency fund.

2. **Debt Snowball** — Pay off debt in a debt snowball method. This consists of paying off debt from smallest to largest — paying the minimum balance on all but the smallest debt. Any extra monies are thrown at the smallest debt until it is gone. When that smallest debt is paid, the monthly payment that was put towards the first paid off debt is then rolled up into the next lowest debt monthly payment. The payments keep rolling into the next lowest debt as each one is paid off. Thus, the debt payments turn into a rolling snowball that gets bigger and bigger. This accelerates the debt payoff substantially and one is now motivated by seeing the progress.

3. **Fully-Funded Emergency Fund** — Save 3–6 months of monthly living expenses for a fully-funded emergency fund.

Now one might assume from reading our prologue that going through the course was that magical point at which life became instantly perfect, right? WRONG!

Turning our finances around was no easy overnight fix and life was not full of roses and rainbows starting on day one. Just trying to get Bob and I on the same page was a journey in itself!

I have learned to appreciate that Bob and I are different. I tend to jump feet-first into

> ## JENSPIRATION
>
> *Hope fuels action and starts when fear no longer rules. Nothing overcomes fear better than taking action.*

things with a ready, FIRE, aim approach, whereas Bob tends to be much more laid back and requires a bit of warming up to new trends.

The differences that once added spice to our life were now causing strife in getting on the same page financially those first few months. It was a case of, "you take the right lane (slow lane) and I'll take the left lane (passing lane for speeders)," with each of us going at our own pace. We hoped we would meet at some point but we weren't sure when or where.

Who could blame us for being on different levels? Bob had left for hockey one evening and had come home to a wife who wanted to change everything we knew to follow a financial plan from some person he had never heard of before. I, on the other hand, wanted to start yesterday because I saw it as a possible financial solution that could lead us to a cure for Robbie.

Overnight, I became consumed with finding out everything I could about financial planning.

It was a huge mistake on my part to assume my change in attitude would come as quickly for my husband.

Rather than giving Bob some time to learn about the plan and warm up to the idea, I made a terrible mistake of talking about this new plan ALL the time those first few months. In doing so, I had turned him off to the idea.

I couldn't fathom how he couldn't be on board and he couldn't grasp the idea of suddenly removing all forms of enjoyment from our lives.

Ultimately Bob reluctantly agreed to give it a try and jumped on the raft, but it took a few months.

So...what important things did we learn about personal finances?

The Dreaded "B" Word: Budget

We discovered that the budget was the most important tool we could possess when it came to controlling our finances.

Early on, however, we both hated the "B" word (budget) and what it stood for. It felt like we were going to be in a living straight-jacket for the rest of our lives. Yuck!

In addition, like many people feel today, the thought of taking the time to sit down and write out a budget was intimidating. How does one even start?

Just finding the right budget tool was stressful.

Our budgeting tool needed to be something easy to use and not some overly complicated spreadsheet that was going to take us forever to try to figure out. After some research, we decided on one that would work for us and went for it.

JENSPIRATION

A budget is the tool to financial freedom! To eliminate debt without a budget, we might as well show up at a marathon 100 pounds overweight, smoking a cigarette, and drinking a beer.

The First Steps to a Budget

In the process of putting together our first budget, we needed to take a look at our past spending habits, how much debt we had, and our current incomes. Let me tell you, that was one eye-opening experience!

First we needed to investigate exactly how much we brought in.

Finding Out What One Really Earns

We hunted down our pay stubs to see what we were actually bringing home. Between the two of us, we made $100,000 annually, yet we were broke. Why was this and how could this be? If we would have heard someone say they made $100,000 and were broke we would have thought that something was terribly wrong with "THOSE people." Yet here we stood, we were one of "THOSE people" that had a six figure income and were broke!

Discovering Where the Heck Money Goes

When it came to finding out where our money was going, we were floored (like most people are when they figure this part of their budget out)! Nearly $1,000 each month was gobbled up at restaurants and fast food drive-thrus. "No way, how could this be?" was our response when we added the numbers up. The vast amounts of thoughtless food spending was astounding.

Here is how our monthly eating out expenses went for us:

Friday: Pizza with family and friends = $50 x 4 = $200

Saturday: Chinese with family and friends = $50 x 4 = $200

Sunday: Mexican with family = $50 x 4 = $200

Weekday: Lunches for Bob and I = $50 x 4 days = $200

Daily: Quick drive thru trips when rushed = $50 x 4 = $200

This didn't include the coffee stops or mindless buying of snacks and whatnot. This was just normal every day monthly expenses.

Where the heck else was our money going?

As far as those $100 charges at places such as Wal-mart, Target, and Home Depot we couldn't even begin to tell you what we had bought when we looked around. It seemed we could never walk out of a store with just the stuff we ran in to get. Between us picking up a few things here and there and the kids getting some $1 items from the dollar section, it was sinking us into debt one dollar at a time.

First Steps to Discovering Debt

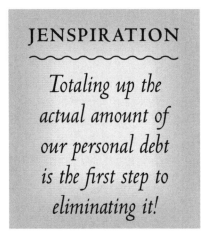

JENSPIRATION

Totaling up the actual amount of our personal debt is the first step to eliminating it!

Along with figuring out how much we spent and earned, we needed to figure out how much debt we owed. Ouch!

Before we could do this however, we needed to look at what debt really was.

Back in the day we only considered our line of credit and credit card as "bad" debt. We knew it was important not to have too much bad debt; however, good debt was okay. How did we know that? Simple. Society continuously teaches us that having "good" debt is not only okay, but encouraged.

Sounds crazy when it is said this way, but when you take a look at the statements below you can see that we have all heard/said similar excuses/rationale:

- We need to have a good credit score. Therefore one has to have debt.

- Everyone knows that several maxed out credit cards is bad, but if we only have one or two cards that is okay.

- Payday loans are BAD if you want to use them long-term, however, if you want to use them short-term, they are convenient and easy.

- If we use credit cards, we are earning free stuff; spend a little more and we'll get increased "rewards."

- Using zero interest loans is like having free money — besides, we ALWAYS pay them back before the promotional interest rate expires.

- One needs to keep those student loans for as long as possible because the interest rates are so low.

- Don't pay off your mortgage because it is a great tax write-off.

What we discovered in going through our journey is that *all debt is bad debt.* "Whatchu talkin' about Willis?" (that is for readers around my age) is what we wanted to say when we first learned this. Could this really be true that all debt is bad?

Hearing this concept for the first time is similar to the story I read as a kid, *The Emperor's New Clothes.* It was the story about a vain emperor who desired to be clothed in the finest garments in all the land. He sought out the finest tailors in the entire kingdom that would make him look good. Tailors were found who offered to weave the emperor a one of a kind magical outfit that was invisible to those unfit for their positions, stupid, or incompetent. Well of course the emperor wanted something that made him look unique and magnificent so he hired the tailors.

Oh how splendid the emperor felt when he finally got to wear his specially made new clothes. Even though he himself could not see the outfit, he didn't want to admit that he couldn't for fear that people would think he was unfit for his position, stupid or incompetent. When he paraded about the kingdom, his subjects raved about how magnificent he looked. He felt very special and proud....that is until a child yelled out the obvious, "But he isn't wearing anything at all!" The emperor was shocked to discover that the magical invisible clothing was not so magical — he was in fact buck naked!

Like the emperor's discovery in finding truth, we too find the truth in the realization that debt no matter how it is disguised is just ugly old debt.

JENSPIRATION

Yes, one CAN escape college free of debt. Encouraging a young person to start off their life with debt is just plain crazy! College is possible without debt.

So what is debt?

Debt includes anything that is owed no matter the interest rate, the type of loan, or how much your net worth is. Examples include:

- Car loans/lease
- Credit card
- Mortgage
- Home equity loan
- Lines of credit
- School loan
- IRS debt
- Medical debt
- Business debt
- Relative/friend loan

As simple as all this sounds, we started to prevail when we finally grasped the fact that ALL debt was *robbing* us versus *causing* us to win like we thought.

For years, debt had unknowingly been commandeering our money AND time. In the process, it was also stealing our peace of mind and our freedom.

From our perspective today, it makes me sad and angry to realize that a large percentage of our society has been deceived into thinking that it is normal that we beg to go into debt and then feel honored when credit is "granted". As with the emperor's story, savvy marketing techniques have clouded the truth. In the case of our debt perceptions, we think that we aren't really borrowing money — we are just getting something when we want/need it and therefore it is not considered debt.

In addition, we have been trained to believe, we can't live without debt.

Believing that we can't live without debt is a myth. Believing that debt brings freedom and joy in life is also a myth. The truth is that we can live without debt if we choose and that debt does cause us to become slaves to the lenders.

Think about it, if we didn't have debt in our lives, think of what we could do and how we would live. We wouldn't be working to pay someone else...we would be working for ourselves.

I hope the next time you hear some of the following statements, you will just shake your head and think of the emperor's story:

- Everyone has some debt.

- We deserve decent things.

- There is no way we can live without debt in this economy.

- We need a credit score therefore we need debt.

If debt is so terrible, why is it so widely accepted as the standard in how we live today?

Simple answer: Debt is all around us — it is easy to get and convenient to use.

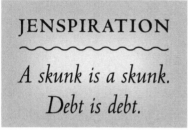

JENSPIRATION

A skunk is a skunk. Debt is debt.

Cash is no longer the preferred payment of choice. Cashiers today have more experience with swiping plastic than making change. Here are some incredible facts about credit cards:

- Dun & Bradstreet released a study that showed we tend to spend 12–18% more when we use a credit card versus when we pay with cash.

- McDonalds did a study that showed we pay 40% more per ticket when we use a credit card over cash.

- Demos released a study that revealed 40% of low-and-middle-income households used credit cards to pay for basic living expenses, such as rent, mortgage bills, groceries, utilities, and/or insurance.

Great media marketing campaigns have led us to believe that we will lead a better life when we use debt. This probably would have sounded crazy to our grandparents, however, with it being all around us today, it has just become the "norm".

Normal causes pain, stress, and heartache. So why is it again that we all want to be normal?

Getting back to our story...

Debt Compartmentalization

When we were ready to look at how much outstanding debt we owed, we discovered the painful truth that we had been compartmentalizing our debt. A little here and a little there didn't seem like much each month, however, when we added up the whole amount, it changed our perspectives. We would go on to see (and be disgusted by) how we had let debt creep into our lives over the years one dollar at a time.

The raw truth we discovered is that we had been sailing on the River of Debt Denial for most of our adult lives.

A Debter's Perspective

How does the River of Debt Denial start? It starts off like a trickle and ends up as a flood for some of us. The River of Debt Denial is well traveled these days by people from all walks of life.

Our own trickle started with our attitudes and language.

We unknowingly had become the "Only Had's" type of people as our debt grew over the years. We ONLY had one credit card. We ONLY had a small line of credit. We ONLY had two small car payments. We ONLY had a 5% mortgage rate.

We couldn't see the whole picture because we were viewing it in small and individual compartments.

It is almost like the "Only Had" language we used gave us the excuse to justify each debt.

As in Bob Harper's book, *The Skinny Rules,* he notes that 60% of our population is now overweight (30% of those being obese). He talks about a recent study where a young girl was asked to show what a portion size was from a jumbo bag of potato chips. *"That's easy,"* she said, upon which she strode to the table, grabbed the entire bag, and walked back to her chair. "That's how much I eat."

Like with obesity, we were the people who "ONLY HAD" SOME potato chips. Why then was the whole bag gone? Honestly, because we mindlessly devoured the whole bag one chip at a time.

The Shocking Experience of Adding Up Debt

Before we started our program, we would have told anyone who asked that we ONLY HAD $18,000 worth of debt.

Back then we ONLY HAD a $3,000 line of credit and we ONLY HAD one credit card with a $15,000 limit. So, for us, our answer to how much debt we owed would have been ~$18,000 — Eighteen Thousand Dollars...ONLY.

When we were ready to start looking at our debt as a whole versus looking at it by compartment, we were STUNNED and even more afraid. Between the $18,000 listed above along with our boat, our vehicle, and our other miscellaneous bills, we found that we owed $48,000 in debt! Forty-Eight Thousand Dollars!!!

Our calculated pay-off for $48,000 was FOUR YEARS. It felt like FOREVER!

I couldn't even say out loud how much we owed when we first began. Just thinking about it would make my breathing become shallow and my body would tense with shame, guilt, and a sense that it was going to be impossible to get out from under.

Because we were so terrified to see the whole picture, we delayed counting both our 401k loans and our second mortgage in our debt picture. The $48,000 was hard enough to fathom...what we really owed took our breath away as the amount seemed incomprehensible.

It took a few months, but finally we were ready to face the real truth on what we owed. We discovered we weren't looking at $18,000 worth of total debt, not even $48,000 worth of total debt...

Nope, we were looking at well over $150,000 in debt...ONE HUNDRED AND FIFTY THOUSAND DOLLARS!!!!! This did NOT include our first mortgage.

JENSPIRATION

Facing your total debt numbers is crucial to finding peace and resolve. Whatever the number is, at the end of the day it is just a number. It isn't a grade on who you are as a person...it is a number. Remind yourself to look at it in this way and soon you might be sleeping better at night.

Talk about being paralyzed with shock and fear at seeing triple digit numbers staring back at us!

Having the courage to face our total debt was one of the most terrifying experiences we've had to face. The distressing part was that no one else had gotten us in this mess; we had brought it upon ourselves.

In meeting with people from all over the country, we find that many of our attitudes and actions back then are the same as what people are facing today. In seeing what my journal entry read the night before we started our first budget, it makes me want to shout to those struggling that they can make it even if they are at rock bottom:

Jen's Journal Entry: March 31ˢᵗ — Feeling panicked about our expenses. With Rob's medical bills, our $2,000 car repairs this past week, and other misc expenses. I am mad that we are at where we are at, but am anxious and determined that we can make this work. This sucks to have to eat in, bring lunches to work, and basically live like a poor person, but I am excited about showing the kids how it should be done. Getting tired of hearing myself get so down anytime money related things *come up...especially when Bob or the kids want to do something fun...I basically go into a panic.*

Our freedom finance journey of living on a budget started on April 1st shortly after Robbie's first hospitalization. Life hasn't been the same since.

~~~~~~~~~~~~~~~~~~~~~~~~~~~~~~~~~~~~~~~

QUESTIONS TO PONDER:

What steps can you take to face your own finances?

Do you know what your WHOLE financial picture looks like?

~~~~~~~~~~~~~~~~~~~~~~~~~~~~~~~~~~~~~~~

JEN'S GEMZ

~~~~~~~~~~~~~~

Live With MOTIVATION!

If you want to conquer fear, don't sit home and think about it. Go out and get busy.

~ Dale Carnegie

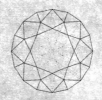

CHAPTER 7

~~~~~~

Frogs in a Frying Pan

Myth: My spouse and I can't get along when it comes to money.

Fact: Couples from all backgrounds have learned to get on the same page when it comes to money.

Stat: Money issues are the number one cause of divorce. ~ Dave Ramsey

What does having financial stress in one's life look like when one is in debt? How can one suddenly just "find" themselves head over heels in financial trouble? Is anyone else having financial troubles or am I alone?

People I meet up with who have asked similar questions can relate to the story of the frog in the frying pan when it comes to living with debt.

You may be wondering what the heck frogs have to do with finances. If so, just hang tight with me for a chapter and I will explain.

The frog starts off in a frying pan of cold water that is slowly heated little by little. Rather than worry about the dangers of being in hot water, the frog decides to happily splash around with his other frog friends. After all, being in a frying pan of water with other frogs sure is better than sitting on some boring rock. Everyone knows that only the boring frogs hang out there. "Besides, they are not having near as much fun on the rock as we are in here," the frog reasons.

"Whew, it is sure getting hot in here." A few of his frog friends complain after a while. "I guess it is a little warm, but what the heck, the other frogs are here with us, let's just stay a little while longer and play."

Eventually the water in the frying pan starts to get steamy; however, because the rise in temperature is slow and gradual, the frog doesn't seem to notice right away.

Over time, the frog continues to play even though he is getting extremely uncomfortable. Why does he do this?

The simple answer is because it feels normal for the frog. It is how he has lived his life and where all his friends are living at as well.

As time goes on the temperature continues to rise and the pain continues to increase. Still the frog chooses to ignore the warning signs and continues splashing about because he sees this as being the norm.

JENSPIRATION

Normal is living one step away from disaster. At 211 degrees the water is hot…at 212 it is boiling. Live with intention and get out of the water.

Then one day, it finally happens, the water temperature hits that inevitable point where it begins to boil.

When this happens, the frog doesn't know what hit him.

He is left feeling helpless and hopeless as his world starts to boil in around him. He can't see his way out and is left wondering, "How the heck did I wake up this morning in this frying pan full of boiling water?" Why is this happening to me?"

For us, it was 17 years of sitting in the frying pan of water. We didn't notice the hot water until it started to boil.

Like the frog, little by little each year, our discomfort slowly increased as we had taken on more debt. Not enough to notice, but just enough to start to feel some moments of discomfort along the way.

JENSPIRATION

Normal is playing on the highway. Intentional living is driving the car.

Living like this feels average when you are in it.

To an outsider, what is coming is obvious. However, much like the frog we weren't inclined to jump out when the pain associated with our debt was so slow coming on.

The world around us seemed to share financial worries akin to our own. During conversations about the economy, our neighbors, friends, family, and coworkers held similar concerns about being able to keep their heads above water when it came to money and finances.

"The car needed tires. The kids' sports teams are going on even MORE out-of-town expensive trips. Peanut butter costs how much? Gas went up again." You could hear the "not again" tones in these types of water cooler discussions.

It seemed to be happening more often as talks of company layoffs, furloughs, pay cuts, and the ever rising costs of living dominated discussions...gloom and doom was all around us.

Not long after our son's first hospital visit, our frying pan of water began to boil. I'm not just talking about a few little bubbles, it got to a wild rolling boil — the kind that makes macaroni seem to dance about. Our finances started to cave in on us. The wounds from living paycheck to paycheck over the years finally began to surface and blister when our life emergency hit. Like the frog in the frying pan, we had helped to facilitate our own demise and there was no rescue crew in sight.

> ## JENSPIRATION
>
> *A speck of hope carries more weight to accomplishing extraordinary things in life versus years of piled up guilt and/or shame. Hope will allow us to leap out of the pan and into the kitchen.*

What should have been the best of financial times in our life turned into a living nightmare.

Over the years, living this way had beaten us into believing this is how it was...simply put, it seemed to be the norm. We didn't want to get out of the frying pan that was destroying our lives; it had become our way of life!

This is how many people in our society live today. The pains of living paycheck to paycheck build up slowly over time. The water in the frying pan doesn't hit boiling until some emergency strikes their lives. If this is the case for you, no doubt you will find yourself waking up in a frying pan full of boiling water asking yourself in stunned disbelief:

- What the heck happened?

- Why is this happening to us?

QUESTIONS TO PONDER:

Are you one of our former frog neighbors still in the frying pan? If so, can you feel the steam building up around you? Does it feel like you are trapped?

(If so, KEEP READING! We got out of the frying pan and so can you!)

JEN'S GEMZ

Live With PERSEVERANCE!

A hero is an ordinary individual who finds the strength to persevere and endure in spite of overwhelming obstacles.

~ Christopher Reeve

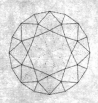

CHAPTER 8

First Steps Felt More Like Stumbles

Myth: The little guy can't get ahead.

Fact: According to Tom Stanley's book, *The Millionaire Next Door*, the majority of millionaires today are made up of ordinary everyday people and NOT the rich and famous as most assume.

Stat: 28% of Americans admit to not paying all their bills on time. ~ 2010 Consumer Financial Literacy Survey

Back to our finance story.

By now, one would think it was like a scenic boat ride into financial paradise. We had our perfect budget and we knew how much debt we had. Now all we had to do was start tracking and using our budget.

All the hard work was done right?

Not! It was like being tossed in a rapidly flowing river with no oars and fast approaching rapids in sight when it came to working with our first budget.

The good news is we learned how to swim fast, even if it didn't look all that pretty.

Communication is Important

One of our first lessons in learning "how to swim" was discovering the hard way that communication was important. Especially since money issues are the number one cause of divorce. It is no wonder that learning how to communicate can take a while to master for some.

By the end of our first week on a budget, I was livid and Bob was wondering what

> **JENSPIRATION**
>
> *There is NEVER a perfect month and life never stays the same so a new budget is needed for each month. With practice, a new budget can be done each month in ~15 minutes.*

the heck happened to his wife. Our disagreement centered around our different levels of understanding of what exactly this new plan of living on a shoestring budget entailed. I was furious and heartbroken when I found a check card transaction for lunch every day of our FIRST week. To me, I saw these transactions as eating away at the opportunity to find a cure for Robbie.

Bob on the other hand didn't see it this way. He only was doing what we both had done in the past by going out for a quick stress reliever lunch with the guys from work. Yikes! Talk about a difference in how we looked at things.

This budget stuff was one thing to see on paper, but quite another to practice.

They were just black and white numbers, why was this not going how we thought? Did we really spend that much on gas and groceries? We only had $12 in our entertainment budget —

shouldn't there be some sort of bonus credit for this? How does one go about getting bonus credit on this program? What, no bonus credits available? Are you kidding?

While those times were difficult to go through, we learned a valuable lesson about the need to communicate when it comes to finances.

Learning Wants Versus Needs

Besides learning how to communicate with each other, we learned to define what our true wants versus our true needs were — especially during our first year. Changing our behaviors was challenging. Even paying attention to the language we used was important to changing our actions.

If you listen closely to the language around us every day, you will hear the term "I NEED" used for things that would NOT have been considered "I NEED" type of items in our grandparents era.

- We NEED to take out a second mortgage to have our house remodeled.

- We NEED a college loan to get an education.

- We NEED to take out a car loan because we NEED reliable transportation.

JENSPIRATION

Debt consolidation companies are a rip off... they don't do anything that you can't do. Save yourself the money and start your own debt elimination program.

In learning how to change our perceptions, we had to reframe our thinking AND our language. Some of the things we thought we "needed" at the beginning of our journey are not even on our "want" list for the most part today. These included:

- Unlimited family entertainment expenses (we were grateful to have the $12 we did for our family of five when we started)

- Cable TV (while we didn't have cable at the time, we had thought about getting it quite a few times)

- Cell phones

- Kids' sports

- Restaurants

- Fast food

- Expensive work clothes

- Car washes (washing by hand can be great family fun time!)

- Newest gadgets

- New reliable cars

- Landscaping products

- Workout gear

- New household items

Think of a person in Uganda looking at the above list. Do you think any of the items would appear on their "I need" list? I highly doubt it. Talk about a perspective change when we see things in a different light.

Learning to say "I don't need" has been incredibly liberating.

Learning to Say No

Another life-altering lesson for us was learning to say "no." We used to associate the word "no" with deprivation. Today we associate it with empowerment.

Teaching ourselves and our kids the meaning of "no" has catapulted us out from under our former dangerous behaviors that would have eventually destroyed our finances and our lives. For being such a small word, it certainly carries a lot of weight, especially in today's society where we are encouraged to have what we want today with no need to pay until tomorrow.

It has been inconvenient at times to tell ourselves NO, but oh so worth it.

Stuff is Just Stuff

Letting our "stuff" go was another meaningful life lesson, one that was hard to learn, but oh so freeing.

Read on....

JENSPIRATION

Having less stuff and being free of debt is better than having lots of "stuff" and no life.

After listening to Dave Ramsey's advice on selling things to get one's finances moving we found ourselves irritated. We thought that was fine for SOME people, but we had NOTHING to sell. It was exasperating to listen to this part of the lesson because it didn't pertain to our situation — or so we thought.

We were $1,000 in the hole the first month of instituting a budget; this, even after we had repeatedly combed through our expenses looking for ways to

cut. How were we going to make this work if we couldn't even meet our monthly expenses?

We looked around for things to sell several times, but couldn't see anything we had of value. Seeing nothing to sell made our $1,000 budget shortage even more frustrating.

Still...even though we didn't see anything to sell and we were frustrated about not having enough in our budget, we still had our goal of getting Robbie out to Denver.

> **JENSPIRATION**
>
> *Goal-setting and striving towards our goals is key to winning.*

Funny how solutions will come to us when we feel trapped and have the hope to think we can fight our way out.

It was at this point that we really started to question what our wants versus our actual needs were.

Admittedly, it was not an easy thing to do.

After inventorying things more carefully and realizing that selling "stuff" was the only way we could immediately picture making our budget work and getting the funds for our son's medical trips, we discovered that we did have some things to sell.

We spotted the electric motor pontoon Bob had bought for my birthday the year before. Could we sell it? The kids loved it and we

> **JENSPIRATION**
>
> *Taking a step back to view where we spend our resources will point us to where our treasures lay.*

were sentimental about it as it had been a birthday present. It didn't seem right to sell.

We talked about it quite a bit and agreed we liked the fact that it would free up some of our monthly cash flow and eliminate some debt if it sold. After hemming and hawing, Bob put it up for sale on Craigslist to see what would happen.

It was our first step in viewing our valuable possessions as "just stuff."

The boat ended up selling on Craigslist within the first two weeks. Even though the kids were bummed, we were elated after it was gone. It sounds kind of strange, but thinking about selling it was much more difficult than actually selling it.

Once the pontoon was gone, we watched as hundreds of dollars from our boat payment were freed from our monthly budget. We were able to pay off our boat loan completely and have an extra $500 left over. Bob and I were surprised at how freeing it felt when it was gone.

What else did we have sitting around? We started to take inventory of our "stuff" with fresh eyes.

What about that old pickup truck we used in the winter? Oh, I don't know. We needed a four-wheel-drive truck because we lived in the country. Selling it just didn't seem smart.

We were okay with letting go of the boat once it was gone; however, our thoughts naturally drifted back into the "that is MINE" mentality. Besides, it needed some work…would anyone even want to buy it in the condition it was in? We were not in a position to sink ANY money into it.

Bob listed it on Craigslist. That, too, sold within two weeks and brought in a few hundred dollars!

After the truck and pontoon sold, we started to get excited about posting more things on Craigslist — it became almost addicting to see what we could find next.

Our eyes started taking in all kinds of things we had to sell. Hey, what about that big compost drum in the backyard that we couldn't give away the year before? Think anyone would like that? Sold on Craigslist within a day.

> **JENSPIRATION**
>
> *Learning to let go of the borrowed treasures we cling to is a basic ingredient to Living Beyond Rich.*

How about that fridge in the garage? Sold in less than an hour. We were on a roll.

When all was said and done, we sold $7,000 worth of items those first few weeks. $5,000 went towards paying off our boat. The other $2,000 was split between our $1,000 emergency fund, and $1000 towards debt. By paying down our debt, it freed up our monthly cash flow which allowed us to come up with a zero-based bare bones budget.

Our biggest lesson in letting stuff go came almost nine months after we started our plan. We sold our hardest material item to let go of. It was our vehicle...the reason it was hard to let go was that it was reliable and we owed more on it than it was worth.

Our vehicle costs were right on the money when it came to the average of what people are paying today.

Average Car Payment – The average monthly vehicle payment sits at around $475 with an overall cost of $26,000 with a 9.6% interest rate on a 6 year loan.

It made us sick when we saw the numbers to demonstrate what our vehicle was actually costing us to drive versus investing it in ourselves. We found that if we had invested that $475 a month over a 30-year period we would have earned:

- **8% Return:** $475 monthly payment x 30 years = ~ $700,000

- **10% Return:** $475 monthly payment x 30 years = ~$1,000,000

- **12% Return:** $475 monthly payment x 30 years = ~ $1,600,000

This is just with one car payment — we had two at one time for many years. Talk about making one ill!

We wanted to sell our vehicle, but we were so upside down on what we owed that it took us several months before we made the decision to list the darn thing. At first, it was difficult to accept selling it for even a $1,000 less than we owed. We realized however that each month we held on to it was costing us another $475, PLUS it was going down in value day by day.

After several months of dropping the price, we disregarded what we owed and listed it for $1,000 less than similarly listed vehicles. It finally sold.

What did it cost us? We owed $21,000 on the vehicle and sold it for $13,000. That left us with an $8,000 debt on something we no longer owned. Even though $8,000 was a lot of money to us, it was a relief to see it sold.

Throughout all this, I will tell you that I was so proud of my husband for letting that vehicle go. If you asked Bob today if it was worth selling our van for $8,000 less than what he owed after being so adamant that we not sell it for even $1,000 less, he would say it definitely was.

Bob's heart and views went through a major overhaul when it came to having "new reliable" vehicles for our family. We can now see the value in buying used cars at a fraction of what they cost new. So what if we need some repairs on occasion, it still is a heck of a lot cheaper than a monthly car payment. Yes, this is coming from a mom with four kids who commutes 90+ miles each day.

Learning that the typical "Millionaire Next Door" also buys used cars emphasized the fact that this was a wise decision going forward for our whole family.

Selling the vehicle was a mental victory in our journey. It also was the first major shift in freeing up money in our penny tight budget.

Since then, it has been liberating to learn how to let go of the material things we used to put so much value on.

In working with clients on setting up their first budgets, I can see in their eyes what we faced not long ago when it comes to letting some things go. I know, I get it. It can be hard to do. I am telling my readers however, that the act of letting stuff go really is empowering when one can see that it is driving them towards the path of financial freedom. By having less, it really gains you more.

QUESTIONS TO PONDER:

Are you letting "stuff" rule your world?

Can you see the benefits of letting things go in order to become free?

PART III
Lessons Learned

JEN'S GEMZ

~~~~~~~~~~~~~~~~~~

Live With PURPOSE!

Success demands singleness of purpose.
~ Vince Lombardi

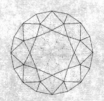

CHAPTER 9

~~~~~

Emergencies Never
Come at Good Times

Myth: Emergencies? Why would anyone antici-
pate those?

Fact: Emergencies WILL strike all of us.

Stat: When Americans encounter an emergency or
unexpected expense, one in four adults without savings
will charge it to a credit card (25%) or take out a loan
(29%), thus taking on or adding to existing debt. About
half will turn to family or friends to borrow the money
(51%), but as many as one in five (21%) will be forced
to neglect their other financial obligations. ~ 2010 Consumer Financial Literacy Survey

~~~~~

I had a friend of mine who used to cue up Louie Armstrong's *It's
a Wonderful World* each morning for his wake up music. You know
the one..."I see trees of green...red roses too. I see 'em bloom for
me and for you. And I think to myself...what a wonderful world."
Ahhh...to hear that deep rich voice paint a picture of what a won-

derful world looks like IS wonderful. Go ahead…hum out a few more bars and then smile.

That song represents what most of us expect our lives to be like ALL the time. Think about it…Louie never sang about being in debt up to your eye sockets and then having so much anxiety and fear built up that you don't know what to do. What a depressing song that would have been to wake up to.

Pastor Bob Merritt, author of *7 Simple Choices for a Better Tomorrow*, put emergencies in perspective when he talked about the hills and valleys in our lifetime. It centered on a bible verse that refers to "WHEN trouble comes our way" NOT "IF trouble comes our way." He went on to clarify that we were never promised that we wouldn't have troubles, instead the bible clearly stated that WHEN trouble comes our way to rely on Him.

What? We must have skipped over that part in the bible. We thought if we were faithful followers, prayed for money fixes, and did good things then we could avoid pain in our lives…wasn't that right?

Pastor Merritt summed it up that we ALL have three phases in our paths when it came to storms entering our lives:

1. **We were either getting ready to head into a storm.**

2. **We were in a storm.**

3. **We were coming out of a storm.**

What an incredible illustration of what true struggles in life look like. Instead of expecting emergencies, we used to feel cheated when emergencies came our way.

How many of us are living our financial life reactively instead of proactively? We don't tend to look for storms…rather, we count on constant sunshine.

In the process of becoming financially free, we discovered how it was worth it was to react proactively versus of reactively when it came to preparing for life to happen.

JENSPIRATION

An emergency fund is a good cure to sleepless nights.

During our 17 years of marriage, Bob and I never had an emergency fund or even a true savings account. Sure, we had money sitting in a bank account, but that was only because we pulled money from of our line of credit. We used to consider this "our money." When we had to actually come up with the money for our $1,000 emergency fund, we realized what really constituted 'our money'.

As silly as it may sound, it was scary to have that $1,000 set aside in a separate savings account that we kept for emergencies only. What if we fell off the wagon and started to go into more debt? We had a 17 year history of "debting." We wanted to make it work and were concerned this may have been too tempting to have around.

The first few months seemed to hold many "emergencies": car tabs, car insurance, school supplies and anything else that we didn't plan for. Each time we would forget to add something into our new monthly budget, it became an "emergency."

We seemed to dip into our emergency fund quite a bit that first year; however, over time we found that our emergencies lessened. Why was this? Because we learned to budget our expenses better and we discovered the value of creating a new budget for each new month since there are never two months that are the same.

Does that mean emergencies never came our way? Absolutely not...we have found that emergencies happen to EVERYONE, including us.

Here are just a few examples of what came our own way....

Two months after we started our finance journey, we squeaked out Robbie's initial overnight visit to Denver. Being able to pay cash for our trip was amazing as it seemed impossible just a few months prior.

> ## JENSPIRATION
>
> *Don't just let life happen, be intentional and prepare for life.*

By the time his second visit which involved a 2 ½ week hospital stay came the following month, we thought we were getting this budget stuff down. We scrimped and were able to tuck money away for his two and a half week hospital stay.

Things don't always go as one plans do they?

A few days before we were scheduled to leave, Bob broke his foot and ruptured/detached his achilles tendon. He had surgery on Thursday and I left with our three kids for Denver on Sunday. I had never driven more than two hours at a time (I used to get lost on occasion going home after we first moved). It was July and we made the 17-hour driving trip from Minnesota to Denver with no air conditioning. Even with all the athletic adventures we've had, I don't think the kids or I had ever sweated so much. Fixing the air conditioning wasn't in our budget and we were committed to make this budget work no matter what.

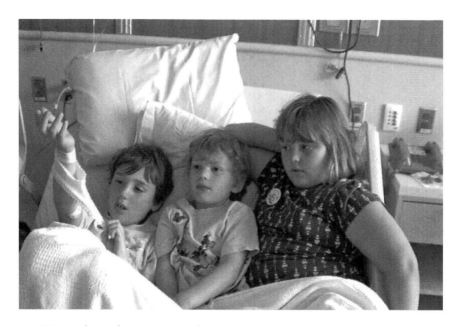

To make a long story short, we survived the emotional hospital stay and the trip out and back. We thought our trauma and drama was over for a while, but soon discovered God has a sense of humor.

We were taken aback to find we were expecting our fourth child shortly after we arrived home (no wonder that I had been tired during our trip).

By the time this unanticipated news came our way, Bob and I finally got on the same page financially. It had taken a few months, but boy was it worth it!

People today are experiencing their own emergencies. Medical situations, divorce, death, job loss, disaster, etc. impact many of us and usually without much warning. Like us, most folks aren't "expecting" these life events to happen and when they do, they're caught off guard.

Having an emergency fund of a few hundred dollars adds a cushion that can transform a flat tire, a broken appliance, or minor setback from an emergency into an inconvenience.

Having a fully-funded emergency fund of 3–6 months can be a welcomed life-line when least expected.

QUESTIONS TO PONDER:

What kind of financial emergencies have you had in your own life?

Were you expecting them? How did you deal with them?

Would having $1000 emergency fund help you to rest easier at night?

JEN'S GEMZ

Live With INTEGRITY!

It's not what we eat but what we digest that makes us strong; not what we gain but what we save that makes us rich; not what we read but what we remember that makes us learned; and not what we profess but what we practice that gives us integrity.

~ Sir Francis Bacon, Sr.

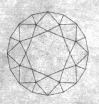

CHAPTER 10

Finding Solutions to Pay Down Debt Faster

Myth: There is no time to work extra jobs.

Fact: We all have an allotted 168 hours per week at our disposal.

Stat: The average American watches approximately 153 hours of TV every month at home. ~ The Nielsen's Three Screen Report, May 2009

I will admit…at $5 a week, we have done our fair share over the years donating to the lottery. The thoughts of that could happen us was always the dream when we were standing in line on Saturday afternoons with our crisp $5 bill that was just begging to be spent.

Coming to the realization that we would have better luck getting struck by lightning over winning the lottery, we choose to focus on making money instead.

When we concentrated on what was possible, workable, and doable we suddenly saw opportunities all around us even in a job market where unemployment rates were at an all time high.

We used to think the only way to get a job was to wait around for places to put up a help wanted posting. The problem with this is that by the time a job is posted, the business most likely has been inundated with applications.

We found success when we became proactive instead of reactive when it came to seeking out extra employment. How did we do this? (The following advice is worth the price of this book tenfold):

- **We searched out places where we could be of service and then made ourselves available.**

Did this really work?

Most definitely it did! In our second year alone, we had ten W-2 forms!

Learning Killer Time Management Skills

We worked full-time and we both had part-time jobs most of the time. This was during a year when we had our fourth baby and continued to travel quite a bit for our son's medical research trips. Between our killer time management skills we put in to use and our new perspective on seeing our weeks as blocks of time opportunities, we kicked butt.

We sought out fill-in positions, temporary positions, and jobs that we could fit within our schedules. Instead of thinking we couldn't possibly work extra hours with our already full schedules, we said "bring it on" and made it work.

How did we do this?

- **Rather than feel overwhelmed by how "busy" we were, we viewed our week in 168 hour 'blocks of opportunities'. By viewing our time in this manner, it allowed us to use our precious hours to the fullest.**

Gaining Perseverance is Golden

JENSPIRATION

Minimum wage pays more than sitting on the couch.

Having excellent time management skills is great, however, what does one do to gain perseverance? This is especially important to know as financial stress can cause emotional and physical exhaustion.

In my book *Living Beyond Awesome*, I tell the story of how the words "Don't Quet (Don't Quit)" came to be tattooed on my ankle. My daughter wrote this misspelled phrase on a sign that my kids had made to cheer me on during my Ironman Triathlon. After being out on the race course for over 14 hours, my body hurt like it never hurt before. At one point when I felt I had given it all I had, I wanted to quit. Never before had I lost my faith like I did during the lowest point in that race.

My daughter's misspelled words of "Don't Quet" (Don't Quit) would eventually become the motto I chanted thousands of times over in my head even when I realized my goals needed to shift. It would be the motto that carried me from the depths of my pain to a victorious finish.

Without knowing it, those two simple words have become our family's mantra when facing life's hurdles. It would be something I silently repeated over and over during our journey to financial freedom.

JENSPIRATION

Goals act as our GPS in life.

Perseverance and Goals Go Hand-in-Hand

I talk more in-depth about goals later on, but I wanted to touch on it here as well as they are so important.

Knowing we have goals gives us vision to see our finish lines. It is what we used when we were diving into working our part-time jobs. Rather than feeling beat down from working so much, we were empowered to use our goals as a tool to take charge of our destiny.

A great example of this was when we found out we were expecting our fourth child. I was so proud of my husband for kicking it into high gear and working his tail off. He took on several janitorial side jobs where he was on his feet just a month after surgery. He would leave the house at 6:00 a.m. for his full-time 10-hour a day job four days a week, then go to his part-time cleaning job which got him home around midnight. He was tired and his heel hurt.

I remember shortly after he started this, his leg wasn't quite up to withstanding pushing an industrial floor sander and he ended up falling a few times. He never complained about this or even when the alarm clock intruded his sleep at 5:00 a.m. each workday morning.

Our goals became our beacon of hope that we could keep going.

I, too, worked four 10-hour days. On Fridays, I would leave at 6:00 a.m. and not get home until 11:00 p.m. because I was working a part-time job at a fitness center. I would be up the next morning at 5:00 a.m. to head out for a few more hours of part-time work.

It was during this busy time that I was feeling awful with the pregnancy and being mom to three active kids. In addition, I developed the HINI flu during my second trimester and had an awful case of plantar fasciitis with a bone spur. It made the half-mile walk up Ramsey Hill (one of the steepest hills in St. Paul that even in my best shape training for Ironman I had never made it half way up running) a bit of a challenge each night however, it also made me appreciate saving $80 a month in parking.

Working through these kinds of times made us stronger not only individually, but also as a couple. Knowing that every one of our sacrifices got us a step closer to our goals made us strive to keep going.

Isn't Extra Income Stealing From Others?

What was so ironic about this is that we felt somewhat guilty for taking on extra jobs at times when people around us were unemployed. We questioned ourselves, is it okay for us to take on these jobs when other people were in what appeared to be more desperate situations?

I tell anyone reading this who may ask themselves the same question to feel free dump any feelings of guilt they may have over this. I can't tell you how many times throughout our journey we encountered people who enjoyed talking the talk, but chose NOT to walk the walk.

An example of this was after returning to work full-time after my maternity leave while at the same time, working a temporary full-time contracting job. At the time our budget was to the penny tight and we were barely squeaking by with paying for Robbie's medical trips.

Being that my heart goes out to those that had been unemployed for long periods of time, I was touched deeply by a particular person I met on this temporarily contracting position.

She had been out of a job for three years and had just about used up all her monies from her retirement and savings accounts. It was just a matter of time before her house would be foreclosed on. I was in tears listening to her story and wanted to help anyway we could.

We ended up finding her some work with my husband's friend that was hiring in the cities for some janitorial work for $12 an hour. When I excitedly gave her the contact info, she turned her nose up at the job. Even though she claimed to have no other means of income, she said the job was too far away, it wasn't worth the pay, and the work wasn't using her master's degree. I couldn't believe it. She was fine with complaining about her situation, however, she wasn't willing to take charge and change it.

Not only did she turn down the cleaning opportunity, but she intentionally cut her hours back from the contracting job from 40 hours a week down to just a few hours after the second week. She wasn't the only one either. By the third week, hardly any of the entire crew was picking up hours. Most of whom were eager to earn money in the beginning had decided that they didn't want to work as summer had come and many had family vacations planned.

Unbelievable! People were losing their houses yet they decided to ditch working and instead go on vacation. Meanwhile, we had four kids at home (one was a newborn), I was working full time, and had foot surgery near this time, yet I was excited to help fill in where they desperately needed help.

Throughout our journey, we have hooked people up with opportunities upon hearing about a dire financial situation. What we discovered is that there are just some people that prefer to whine versus take hold of opportunities given to them. So, it no longer shocks me to hear people openly discuss their financial woes, yet they are holding a $7 beer in their hands and declining to work for $10 an hour.

So if you are feeling guilty about "taking hours from some-one else", believe me when I say there will always be complain-ers that choose not to act no matter what. It is the ones that grab the bull by the horns that will succeed.

One of Our Best Jobs

One of our best jobs we had was delivering pizzas. I chuckle as I write this because of all the jobs we did, delivering pizzas was the one job Bob was ADAMENT that we NOT do.

Since delivering pizzas seemed like an easy way to earn money, I was "nicely persistent" in bringing it up several times in the beginning of our journey. Each time, Bob would silently shake his head no. The next time the topic of earning money came up, I would bring it up again like it was this great new idea. The same silent answer of no was given each time.

Why did I keep suggesting it? Well...I thought perhaps my better half didn't hear or remember the times I had suggested and assumed I was doing a great service by bringing it up each time.

Come to find out…he actually did hear it and remembered it every darn time I brought it up!

My patient husband finally looked at me one day after one of my gentle suggestions and pointedly said, "Jen, there is one thing I will NOT do to earn extra money and that is deliver pizzas." I stopped bringing up the subject after that.

After Remy was born just about a year after we started, I was up getting lawnmower gas with the kids and noticed a local pizza shop under construction. With four kids in tow, carrying a tank of gas in my casual summer wardrobe of shorts and a tank top, I went over to seek out who was in the shop. Lo and behold, the manager was there. I told him outright that my husband and I were interested in part-time work. He interviewed "us" on the spot.

When we pulled up in the driveway 45 minutes later, Bob was there waiting for the lawnmower gas.

Handing over the gas can, I gave him a big kiss and enthusiastically said, "GUESS WHAT honey? (long pause, big smile waiting for him trying to guess the great news) WE just got hired to deliver pizzas." My awesome husband who had been so adamant a few months earlier looked at me with a big grin and said, "That is GREAT sweetie. When do we start?"

Why the change of heart from a few months earlier?

By this time, we were on the same page and had the same goals. My admiration for my husband grew even greater after he took this on.

So, at the ages of 40 and 47, with a newborn and three other kids at home, Bob and I donned our pizza delivery uniforms and started showing up at our startled neighbors' homes. Most smiled, however, some looked at us like we were crazy.

Our pizza delivery jobs actually influenced several people without us knowing it.

One of the couples that we worked with knew our story of working to become financially free. They were engaged and had their dream wedding that included 300+ guests, an overseas honeymoon, and an elaborate reception scheduled for the following year.

To our total surprise, this adventurous young couple decided to cancel their dream wedding. Instead they used the money they would have spent to pay down their student loans. While we were excited for them, quite honestly, we were a little taken back that they would go to such extremes. What happened to this adventurous young couple?

They ended up being married a few months sooner in an intimate local wedding with a few dozen of their closest friends and family surrounding them. Their wedding was beautiful! By cutting back and paying down their debt they were able to buy a house they could easily afford and save up for their ultimate dream of owning their own franchise that they are planning to buy in the very near future. We are so proud of them!

So, while I can't say that standing outside carrying a sidewalk pizza advertisement sign in our small town for $7.25 an hour was the highlight of my life, I will say just like this couple, the thought of becoming debt free faster was joyful.

Besides, we were earning $7.25 more than sitting on the couch watching TV, getting great exercise and getting to listen to inspiring podcasts while working towards our own dream.

Ways of Earning Extra Income

Here are some of the ways we earned extra income to drive down our debt:

- Janitorial

- Pizza delivery

- Contracted administrative assistant

- Seasonal work

- Temporary office help

- Cash side jobs

- Buying and selling cars

- Fitness center staff

- Research studies (not related to Robbie's medical condition – it involved Bob and I)

What are some other low cost easy ideas to get you brainstorming for your own extra income?

- Landscaping (a lawnmower will do)

- Babysitting (consider nights and weekends — people need care all hours of the day)

- Elderly care

- Pet sitting

- Dog walking

JENSPIRATION

When looking for ways to earn income remember to ask, ask, ask, and then ask some more. Look for opportunities where you can be of service and then serve.

- Window washing

- House cleaning

- House sitting

- Tutoring

- Photography

- Coaching

Using Time Intentionally

As mentioned above, we used our time very intentionally. This helped us not only find more ways to bring in income, but also kept our priorities in line while propelling us forward. One of those priorities was for either Bob or I to always be with the kids outside our normal full-time jobs. Sure it was tempting at times to have both of us pulling down extra money during the same time, however, by setting it as an intentional priority; we found solutions for us to make it work.

Our intentional use of time was used in multiple areas of our life, including family, church, friends, work, and ourselves. We cut things such as TV and wandering around at the shopping mall out to make room for the important things in our life.

An example of this intentional time management during this period in our lives centered around our important and valued family time.

Saturday evenings were reserved for our treasured nights as a family. We went to church and then came home to have popcorn and watch movies while snuggled up together.

Sunday mornings were lazy days for all of us. We slept in and did our best to relax. I remember some mornings just wishing the clock would stop as I lay snuggled next to Bob. In his arms I felt safe, cherished and loved. We talked about our dreams and how the kids did during the week while we enjoyed the peace and quiet in each other's company.

Neither of us dared to think about how quickly the work week would begin as we'd be apart for another five days/nights. It was easier to appreciate the time we had together as a couple. Although we didn't see each other much during certain periods of our journey, it made our marriage stronger as we were both working toward the same goals and shared the same dreams and prayers.

Sunday afternoons were spent hanging out in the yard or going to the park with a packed snack. Even though it didn't appear we were "doing anything" we were in fact being intentional about spending our time, energies, and focus with each other.

Kids Can Learn Value of Time and Money Too

Besides learning as a family to appreciate our time together, our kids experienced firsthand the value of staying out of debt as they learned that not only their time was of value, but each dollar earned was worth something as well. When they wanted to buy something and didn't have the money, they looked for ways to earn money outside our home. They have gotten very good at it seeking out opportunities on their own. Extremely cool!

Each Dollar Earned Counted

By paying down our debt as money came in, it kept us in line for not having that "extra" money "absorbed somewhere" in the budget. It also kept us jazzed and motivated to watch our debt melt with each dollar put towards it.

The Value of Money

JENSPIRATION

Placing an hourly wage value on purchases will lead to wise spending.

Besides bringing in extra income, our part-time jobs made us look closely at how we spent our money.

Instead of looking at something as ONLY $8, we now looked at it as one hour of work. The $20 McDonald's drive-thru visit was now three hours of taxed work. Suddenly, those fries and soft drinks didn't look as appetizing, the drive-thru wasn't as convenient, and the value meal wasn't all that valuable.

When we started to view things this way, it gave us a whole new outlook on the value of money. Items were not so easily tossed in our shopping cart.

Letting kids Fail In Order to Grow and Appreciate

As a bonus, our children discovered they needed to save for the things they wanted because mom and dad were done buying treats for them every time we went to the store. Having to spend their own money has transformed them into becoming savvy shoppers. They have come to learn the value of buying used compared to buying new.

In wanting our children to learn through real life experiences, we intentionally let our kids fail when it came to making decisions on some of their purchases. While it was difficult at times to remain silent as we watched their hard earned money being forked over for some cheap breakable toy, it proved to be worth it in the long run. These failures taught our kids more than any preaching ever would have.

When we did have something extra it truly was a treat. A great example of this was when we splurged on our "payments to Robbie" for our trips out to Denver. Robbie, being our analytical child, made a deal with us that for $5, a book, and a happy meal at the airport, he would continue in the diabetes study. He said this was payment for his "pain and suffering" (yep, that is our lawyer).

Funny, you wouldn't give a second glance at seeing a very pregnant mom and her son eating at the airport. I am telling you though, that happy meal was probably the most appreciated meal that McDonalds ever sold.

Finding Inspiration Is Essential

> ## JENSPIRATION
> ~~~~~~~~~~~
>
> *Having a goal takes us from running away from something to running TO something. Goals are a key ingredient to achieving a Life Beyond Awesome.*

I remember during our more crazy times when Bob was gone each night of the week and I had my part time job where I was on my feet (we were both working full-time), I would sit on the couch at night and dream. I was huge, pregnant, tired, and my foot throbbed in pain each night from plantar fasciitis, a bone spur, and from walking in worn out dress-heeled shoes during my 10-hour days. My body would melt into the couch cushions after dinner. With our kids playing with their Legos nearby, we listened to Dave Ramsey and Dan Miller podcasts as they spoke wisdom, hope, and encouragement into our lives each night.

Occasionally, I would get lost in thought while dreaming of what life would be like when we hit our goals during those 45-minute episodes. Thinking I was the only one listening, our kids would remind me with their comments that they were indeed listening as well. It was hilarious to me that at ages 9-, 7-, and 5-years-old they came to know the answers for some of the questions that came up. When someone called in with a credit card question to Dave Ramsey, occasionally I would hear a tsking noise as if to say, "They don't know what they are in for."

On Fridays, my eyes would swell with emotion when people would call in to Dave Ramsey's show to tell their debt-free story and then scream at the top of their lungs, "I'm DEBT FREEE!" When the shouts of "We're debt free!" were heard over the speakers, the kids and I yelled it along with them.

Each time we would hear a caller screaming "We're debt free," I would visualize our family reaching the day when we could scream the same. The yearning for that day was felt EVERY DAY along our freedom journey and will continue for us until that day comes in the not so distant future.

It reaffirmed that our daily sacrifices that were temporarily inconveniences for our family was worth it in the long run.

Learning What an Emotional Job Loss Feels Like

Like numerous employees today I never thought my job would be downsized. My former "totally secure job" was eliminated when the clinic I had worked at for 14 years closed its doors after being in business since the mid 1970's. Having gone from being so needed to not being needed at all was a blow not only financially, but personally as well.

While seeking employment was stressful, we had faith it would work out if we continued to move forward and learn along the way.

Even with faith however, it didn't always stop me from letting my mind wander to scenes of what our future would look like if things didn't turn out. How long would we make it before we lost our house? Would I ever be able to find work? How would this impact our kids?

Emotional Keys to Landing a Job

Keeping these thoughts at bay and instead focusing on keeping my emotional state positive was imperative. Why does this stuff matter?

Because people's emotional state will be transparent during the interview process. If someone is lacking in confidence, bitter about their situation, and/or just an overall downer type person, it will be readily apparent. If someone is positive, confident, and joyful, it will show through their attitude, body language, and discussion.

Confidence, persistence and taking action are keys for success.

If you are reading this with raised eyebrows, wondering how one can be confident during these times, I want to say I get it. The thought is almost counterintuitive when one is deep down terrified at the thought of losing their security, their homes, and/or their savings.

So what is the key to being confident?

- **Practice ACTING confident and you will BECOME confident.**

What was my own final outcome after ACTING confident, being persistent and taking action?

Even in an economy where unemployment rates were so high, three solid job offers were presented me that included everything I asked for. This was after I treated looking for a job like a part-time job — one that I took very seriously. Each day I consistently spent 2–3 hours for research, preparation, application submissions, and follow-through. In the end, the effort definitely paid off.

In addition to the job offers, there were several first and second interviews pending. One place even asked that I come in to interview after I told them they weren't in the running and I didn't have the time. They called me a few times to see if they could possibly find a time that was convenient for me to come in just to talk. It seemed crazy that a place would do this, however, I found the more confident I became, the more people sought me out.

Learning About 401k Loans the Hard Way

To add to the stress of losing my job, my 401k loan became due. Wow, we never even considered this possibility when we had borrowed from ourselves. Yikes! The thought of being able to pay it back seemed impossible, however, we kept pushing to put every extra dime we saved and earned towards our goal.

Going forward a few months, by the skin of our chinny chin chins, we were able to pay off our 401k loan in full a few days before it came due.

Why did I put this note under the pay down your debt faster chapter?

Because borrowing from our 401k loans almost turned out to be one of our most expensive lessons. If we hadn't been able to pay it back, we would have lost out on 40% of the 401k in taxes and penalties. It was a great relief for our money to go back to where it rightly belonged in the first place — into our retirement fund.

The whole job loss experience taught us that the thought that we can borrow on our 401k because we are never going leave our jobs someday is a complete myth.

We have come to understand that we will ALL leave our jobs someday whether it is due to leaving on our own, being let go, or through the act of an injury or dying. That is a 100% guarantee.

QUESTIONS TO PONDER:

What skills, abilities, knowledge, experience and passions can you use to bring in extra income?

What actions are you taking TODAY to reach to your financial goals?

JEN'S GEMZ

Live With RESILIENCE!

Character cannot be developed in ease and quiet. Only through experience of trial and suffering can the soul be strengthened, ambition inspired, and success achieved.

~ Helen Keller

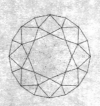

CHAPTER 11

〜〜〜

Pride: a Hurdle to Overcome

Myth: Money is magical and mystical...it will always be there.

Fact: Money is finite.

Stat: 30% of Americans have no savings. ~ 2010 Consumer Financial Literacy Survey

〜〜〜

Learning to let go of pride WILL help you on your journey.

When I was pregnant with our first child, I was very prideful about NOT being treated like I was a pregnant lady (by the time our fourth one came, I was all about being treated like a preggo)! I had been a national weightlifting champion and a women's professional football player (long story, but I had to give up my "football career" when I got over the fact that we were having our first child). Being treated like a pregnant lady in my mind was admitting weakness and I was definitely NOT okay with that.

When I was about 9 months along after working out at the gym as I was stubbornly trying to stay in football shape (I squatted 220 lbs for 3 sets of 1 the night Maggie was born — quite hilarious to see the looks from a few men that I am sure thought I was going to deliver right there and then) my husband Bob made a huge mistake. His blunder came when he tried to drop me off at the door of the movie theater. I was outraged. I turned to him and said, "Bob, that is it! I will NOT be treated like a preggo... who do you think you are trying to treat me like one? What do you think you are trying to do to me?" My very loving husband looked at me and said, "Jen, I always drop you off at the entrance of anywhere we go." Oh, he was right, he did drop me off wherever we went I suddenly remembered. I went from being mad to being a bit embarrassed at my outburst.

Why did these emotions take over (besides the excuse of hormones)? Pride. Pride was preventing me from being able to accept his generosity. It was embarrassing to be offered help and it was hard to accept.

We also had a mountain of pride when we started this journey. While it felt great to hang onto in the beginning, we learned that if we loosened our reigns on it, we'd be able to evolve into the people were meant to be.

JENSPIRATION

Even the strongest and most powerful people in the world are only human and therefore not invincible. Sing the song or read the comic book all you want; I'm here to tell you that you're not ever going to possess infinite supernatural power — we all need a little help and guidance now and again.

Setting aside pride reminds me of a great lesson a friend shared with me recently before she passed away.

Kathleen was one of the most independent persons I had ever known. She was a feisty no-nonsense nurse who had raised a daughter on her own. When you looked up the word independent, you might as well just put her name down as it described her perfectly.

I was saddened to learn she had a stage-4 type of cancer. When I asked if she was doing okay, she shared an incredible lesson she had learned on her journey.

This feisty independent woman who didn't want people to know she had cancer a few months before said these words. "You know Jen, I have an incredible set of friends that I have come to rely on." My eyebrows shot up. Certainly this was not the same stubborn person I had known. She was a person who would have scoffed at help from friends not long ago.

She continued, "I have learned that if you don't let people help sometimes, then you will never let them bring out the best in themselves and discover their true potential." Wow, that blew me away. How true it is and I was honored and humbled to have gotten to see her. I said a prayer of thanks that God had changed her heart to let people help and that she would stay strong on her journey.

Her words of wisdom still ring true for me today when we struggle and/or see others struggling — "How will others know their true potential if we don't let them help sometimes."

Pride is not easy for any of us. In all honesty, it is something that Bob and I continue to struggle with.

A great example of learning to let go of pride the hard way came early on in our journey. A colleague and dear friend who has a huge heart offered to help us fund our medical research trips. I ended up throwing his kind offer back at him in a firm, but gentle way.

Dr. Uma Valeti came into my office one afternoon and said, "Jen, my wife and I want to help you and your son with your trips to Colorado. Will you let us use some of our frequent flyer miles to help with your trips?" The best way to describe my reaction was that I panicked. I was beyond grateful and appreciative that he had made this generous offer. However, I was stumbling over a mountain of pride. My immediate reaction was a definite "Thank you, but we are fine. I can't accept your generous offer." I didn't want to hurt his feelings, but it was my knee-jerk reaction that we couldn't let anyone help us.

"Jen," he stubbornly continued, "why won't you let me help you?" By this time, I was frantically waving my hand no with a smile as I shook my head, "I just can't. You are beyond wonderful to offer, but we just can't." He argued with me a bit more, but I shooed him out the door with a thank you, a goodbye wave, and a smile.

When Bob and I looked over our budget for that month, we were stressed. There wasn't any wiggle room to afford the airfare for Robbie's trip. It was early on in our journey and we were still extremely tight on our finances. We talked about it and prayed about it.

We discussed driving to Robbie's out of state doctor's appointment rather than flying, but came to the conclusion that it wasn't cost-effective. In addition, I had no vacation left to use at work. It had already been used it up for his previous 2-1/2 week Denver hospital stay.

JENSPIRATION

Continuously searching for alternative solutions is key to getting past our barriers.

After a few days, I reluctantly put my pride aside and sought Uma out. "Uma, Bob and I would be very grateful to take you up on your generous offer ONLY if it is not a hassle and ONLY if you truly have enough air miles to donate." His smile couldn't have been bigger as he answered "Of course!"

To put our pride aside and accept someone's help was extremely difficult. The fear of accepting a helping hand from someone was humbling. It was hard to trust and accepting help made us feel like we were failing. Did we love to help other people? YES, but to us it was different being on the accepting end.

Uma and his wife went on to use their frequent flier miles for 3 of our 16 trips out to Denver. He made it clear that we were just to ask and we would receive. Our family is forever grateful for his kindheartedness, compassion, and stubbornness. What amazing friends they are.

My wish for all who read this is that everyone will get to experience the friendship of someone like Uma and his wife. Also, my hope is that if pride is preventing anyone from getting to where they strive to be that they give it a toss out the window, be willing to seek help out, and accept help when needed.

Letting go of pride may seem counterintuitive; however, it will make your journey easier when you do.

QUESTIONS TO PONDER:

Are there areas in your life where pride is causing you to stumble?

How will overcoming prideful issues help you in your quest to financial freedom?

JEN'S GEMZ

Live With GENEROSITY!

We are rich only through what we give, and poor only through what we refuse.

~ Ralph Waldo Emerson

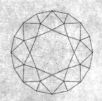

CHAPTER 12

Goals – Keeping the End in Mind Will Drive You to Success

Myth: I don't need to worry about retirement, that is years away.

Fact: If you don't have a target to aim at, you'll hit it every time!

Stat: 33% of Americans do not put any part of their annual household income towards retirement. ~ 2010 Consumer Financial Literacy Survey

Wouldn't it be nice if life was like those moving sidewalks at the airport? We just hop on and it carries us to our destination with no bumps along the way. No worries...just wave and smile as we go.

Don't we find that life seems to be more like the passenger who needs to runs past 20 gates to catch an airplane that has its doors closing in 30 seconds? Why all the work we wonder? Wouldn't the escalator be more pleasant we want to grumble? Yes, it certainly would be...however, if we want to get on the plane we best stop grumbling and start running.

Running to take action is imperative when we want to transform not only our financial lives, but our overall lives as well.

An example of this is American's trending rates of obesity. Similar to paying off debt, the same struggles and concepts exist between paying off debt and weight loss.

For years, I hated how much my bathroom scale read and, much like our former approach to finances, used many excuses to avoid dealing with it. I had ALL the excuses in the world (low thyroid, busy mom, work full-time, this is the way I am made, etc.). Blaming my weight on excuses didn't help me lose one single pound over the years.

In my mind, by exercising I thought it was good enough, even though I was not losing any weight. The frustration and negative self accusations poisoned further attempts and was, no doubt, one of the many reasons my efforts resulted in failure.

Like a myriad of people today, the vicious cycle of trying and then quitting when quick results don't appear was normal. Why even bother trying when the task is overwhelming and seems impossible we think.

Thankfully, the day came when I was ready to put a stake in the ground and admit that all was not what I had thought it was.

> **JENSPIRATION**
>
> *Finances and weight loss have many similarities. Both cause feelings of guilt, shame, anger, and denial. Ditch the negative and go for the positive.*

There was one particular picture my daughter had taken of me that was very painful to see. Could that really be me? The person in the picture certainly didn't match the picture I had of myself, in my head. I didn't like what I saw or enjoy how I felt. I knew right then I had to make a change and soon, as I not only looked terrible, but knew my health was dependent on my making changes.

The problem was that I wasn't equipped with the knowledge, the support mechanism, or the plan to succeed on my own. It was obvious that if I ate less and exercised more I would lose weight, but the thought of that "actually" happening at the time, seemed impossible. I was mentally and emotionally trained to fail rather than succeed and therefore was skeptical.

Success came my way once I admitted my health was deteriorating, I wanted a better life, and I needed help.

I took action by finding a plan that worked for others and then made a commitment to stay on it. I then set my goals and found the support I needed to continue on my journey.

I lost 60 pounds in just a few short months after having failed for years.

At my starting point, I was so out of shape that I couldn't run more than two blocks. A few months into the plan I went on to run my first marathon. Fast forward and since my weight loss, I completed three marathons, several triathlons, and one Ironman Triathlon.

Ignoring the problem and using excuses didn't melt the pounds off, make me stronger, or increase my cardio abilities. By taking action, using a plan, setting my goals, and finding ways to sustain momentum I became successful in my weight loss journey.

JENSPIRATION

Imperfection is a part of life...embrace it, learn from it, and triumph.

Why then do so many of us fail even with taking action and using a plan?

In observing those who are driven yet continue to fall short, I have found one thing to be true. Those who don't learn to forgive themselves for goofing up will most definitely be unsuccessful. For my weight loss success, I learned that each new meal was a new opportunity to strive to do my best no matter what happened in the past.

These same keys held true in our finance journey as well. Besides the above, what was another tool we credit to our success that will help you accomplish great things as well?

Using Goals is Powerful

I've been blessed to have accomplished some incredible feats in my life; after starting with only a broomstick, I became an Olympic style weightlifting champion and despite having no experience and starting with a blank page, I became an author. I'm no genius but I am well versed in using goals as a method for achieving great things.

The simple task of creating written goals puts us 99% ahead of those that don't. We most definitely go further in life when we have targets to shoot for. It makes getting to where we want to go easier and faster than trying to muddle through with no destination of where we are going.

The truth is that the act of taking action to reach our goals is a success in itself. Sometimes people think that goals have to remain the same no matter what...this is hogwash.

JENSPIRATION

Goals are the light through dark times...use the light they offer and get after them.

Successful people know the importance of continuously assessing and realigning their priorities and goals on a regular basis.

When we realize that our paths in life will never be continuously straight, we can then acknowledge that our goals can be changed as our perspectives, situations, and priorities change.

The analogy of setting a goal to finish a marathon within a certain timeframe on a certain day is a great example of a goal that sometimes needs to change. If we set a timeline to finish in, but our time is a little off, in the end who cares, we still completed a marathon and are better off than those who never took those first steps.

Learning to view our failures as learning how to win opportunities is empowering. When we look at our failures as opportunities to learn how to win, it gives us permission to release any feelings of guilt we may incur when we need to adjust our goals.

On another note, I guarantee my readers that the people who continuously learn to adapt to life's twists and turns are those who are wise enough to realize that it is not only the end goal we should be happy with, it is the process in itself we should enjoy as well.

Goals Push Us

Much like many people who struggle with weight issues or with finances, being in the grey zone of indecision and complicity is exhausting and stressful.

In our earlier years, we tried to stay on a budget but failed because we never had clearly defined written goals. Having clearly defined goals has encouraged us to stretch outside of our comfort zones to achieve what once was considered the impossible.

Using goals to make the impossible possible has been proven time and time again amongst successful people. Along with using goals we learned another important tool available for us...our attitude.

While we hit some pretty huge walls in our journey, we learned that "claiming" and not "blaming" has led us to achieving abundant amounts of success.

An example of this was during the times when our poor financial situation had worn us down to the point where many of our thoughts and emotions revolved around money and the lack of it versus how far we had come. It was during these rough

JENSPIRATION

Martyrs don't become successful; they become skilled at whining about being miserable.

times that we needed to consciously choose to fight or continue to stay in the comforts of the "martyr zone."

In all reality, it didn't matter that those around us were complaining about the economy being in the tank. Worrying about our finances didn't pay our bills. The facts were still the facts no matter what the world around us looked like.

Continuously seeking out solutions and claiming self responsibility allowed us to continue to move forward. Reaching our destination required us to keep the end in mind to get us to where we wanted to go and to become who we wanted to be.

Striving towards our goals, positive attitudes, and perseverance allowed us to reach our destination.

Our Current Financial Goals

> ## JENSPIRATION
>
> *Goals are one of our most powerful tools to achieving greatness. They don't discriminate and they are free to all.*

So what are some of our current financial goals?

After we complete our second step of paying off debt, we will save for a 3–6 month emergency fund. After that we are planning to save for a "reward" Disney-type vacation celebration with our kids. This vacation will serve to memorialize how goal setting, sacrifice, hard work and dedication can get us to where we want to be.

After these steps are done, we will start on a new plan for our future. Yes, we know where we want to go.

- **We will contribute 15% each towards our retirement.**

- **We will save for our kids 'college funds.**

- **We will pay off our house in the next 7–12 years.**

We can't wait. The above goals were something we thought unattainable in our former life.

Our journey has transformed us from being folks who thought we could never get out from under debt to being folks who know no challenge is too great — it's so freeing! Our story is proof that it is NEVER too late to TRANSFORM who we are.

How does one start a transformation process?

Your journey of transformation starts with the acknowledgement that change is needed. Once that step is taken, your journey can begin.

QUESTIONS TO PONDER:

How will your life play out?

Are you using goals and solutions to transform your life into the life you were meant to live?

PART IV
Keys to Living Beyond Rich

JEN'S GEMZ

Live With CONTENTMENT!

Content makes poor men rich; discontent makes rich men poor.

~ Benjamin Franklin

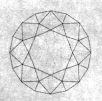

CHAPTER 13

Transformation is a Process — A Process of Changing the Heart

Myth: I don't have time to learn finances.

Fact: Learning how to take control over your finances takes less time to learn than the average amount of TV a person watches in a week.

Stat: Most behavior experts agree that it takes about 21 days to form a new habit.

Glorious miracles of transformation continuously surround us in nature each day. Storm clouds that hold tragedy and chaos can transform into brilliant bright blue skies that contain the sun's warmth for us to take pleasure in. A caterpillar's ability to transform into a beautiful free flying butterfly. Seeds that transform into tall shady trees that give us relief on a hot day. These are every day transformations that we unknowingly benefit from daily.

What a great sense of wonderment to realize people can transform as well. It is our choice whether we want to have these transformations be positive or negative.

A story of contrasting transformation took place literally the same month that we hit our rock bottom financially. An acquaintance of ours had an extremely large financial windfall come their way all at once. Like us, they had been living paycheck to paycheck throughout the years.

It has been attention-grabbing to see how both of our families have progressed throughout the same time period. One couple had a pot of gold come their way and the other couple (us) were starting out in pain and stress at the bottom of 'Debt Mountain'. Surely one would think the ones with the pot of gold would come out ahead right? Shockingly, not so.

Our journeys of transformation took us on completely different paths.

Within a month, our acquaintances had 80% of their financial windfall spent! They paid cash for a house they found on a whim, bought a new vehicle, and furnished their new house from top to bottom.

It used to be hard to understand how lottery winners could ever go broke and their lives fall apart. Some get divorced, run out of money, and their relationship with finances ends up being disastrous. Their level of lifestyles increase and they end up broke and more in debt than before they won the lottery.

We use to think lottery winners were "lucky" to have had such great fortunes come their way. Today, the word "lucky" doesn't describe what we feel when reading about some of their despairing situations.

In working our way to the top, our perspectives and attitudes have transformed in many ways.

Before we started, we used to be the hamster in the wheel — spinning, but not getting anywhere. We worked hard, we paid our bills, gave when we could, and paid our taxes. We worked harder at times, but still didn't get ahead...in fact, it felt like we got farther behind.

Finding Contentment

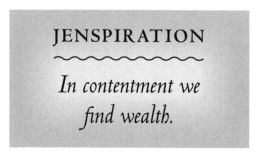

JENSPIRATION

In contentment we find wealth.

Like many today, we used to fill our days with chasing after things to fill our desires. We used rainy days, days we were tired, and/or days we were just bored as excuses to spend our way to finding short term happiness. Many times it wasn't the bigger expense items that got us into trouble; it was those $10 to $20 items that we were constantly searching for and/or the mindless impulse purchases.

Take a look around the next time you are out shopping. What are people purchasing? When one steps back and looks at the big picture, it is fascinating to take notice of what people are actually buying. Foreclosures and unemployment may be at an all time high, however, finding a parking space at the mall can be a challenge.

Learning how to find contentment along the way has been instrumental to our family learning how to live beyond rich.

It has been a powerful process to see how our own personal needs and wants have evolved throughout this journey. Many things we desired and NEEDED in the past have now become things that we can't even imagine wanting today. Our wants no longer control our actions as they once did.

It has been extremely freeing to have those burning intense material desires lessen over time due to this experience.

Becoming Intentional Givers

With having our material desires lessen, our desire to learn to become intentional givers has increased.

We used to think we were good givers. If someone was raising money for something or when the plate was passed around at church we would toss in $20. We enjoyed it very much, yet, we never were intentional with our giving. We just gave what we thought we had left over. It's fine for some people to be gener-ous givers, but get real, we can't afford to be. Besides, there would always be other people to give and do more than us right?

JENSPIRATION

Learning to be generous with our resources leads to a life of abundance. Living with an open hand not only allows money out, but also allows money in.

In studying people, we found that the most joyful and successful people are great givers of their time, talents, and/or money. Seeing this, we wanted the same however, getting our budget to match our hearts took time and discipline.

When we were $1,000 behind in our first monthly budget, it seemed impossible to afford to donate to any type of charities. We reluctantly agreed to give it a try and made an intentional commitment to start with 1% and increase our giving each month until we hit our goal of 10%. In addition, we started to give more of our time and talents.

JENSPIRATION

Give my money to the bank or give it to charity? Which is better? Charity and mortgage interests have the same tax benefits. Check out this great example taken from Dave Ramsey:

If you have a $200,000 mortgage loan at 5%, you're paying $10,000 in interest.

- If you earned $70,000 and deducted that interest on your tax return, you'd save $2500.

- That means you're paying the bank $10,000 in order to reduce your taxes by $2500.

Think about that for a second. . .you are sending the bank $10,000 in order to avoid paying the government $2,500.

There were months, when we were counting pennies, that charity became a hot topic between Bob and me. The thought of getting to 10% seemed impossible...it truly did. After the hot topic was discussed at length, it was agreed on that we continue on our mission of getting to our 10% goal by increasing it little by little each month.

Along the way, we reminded ourselves that we had a roof over our heads, food, transportation, and clothing. Just these things alone would put us in top 1 percent of the wealthiest in the world. Wow, isn't that amazing to think that just based on these basic necessities that we all expect in our society that this puts many of us in that same category?

Even knowing this, it was a bit scary to continue to have faith that if we continued to give more and more that our budget would continue to work each month. It seemed unattainable to continue to squeeze out more each month, but we found that we were able to when we put our faith into action.

At exactly our two-year mark, I am proud to say that we did hit our goal of giving 10%. We also became regular volunteers at our church and found more time to foster relationships. Wow, the impossible became possible as our hearts and perceptions on giving took on a major overhaul.

JENSPIRATION

Vanilla ain't a color in the rainbow. If you want to find awesomeness in life, avoid normal and take action to do things extraordinary.

To experience the joy of being intentional givers has been incredibly cool for Bob and I, and an awesome experience for our kids.

The Ripple Effect of Giving

We know our family cannot possibly reach each and every person in need in this world. However, Dave Ramsey demonstrated to us the difference that one family can make when we become intentional with not only our finances, but also our life. He caused the ripple effect that got our family on board when it came to getting our finances (and life) in order.

Our family continues that ripple effect through our kids and has now started our own ripple effects to others through sharing our story. We know those ripples will continue through others as they did through our family.

Just think...with enough ripples, it could cause a wave that would call for less reliance on things such as government programs and reach more people in dire straits worldwide. That may sound corny to some, but it is true.

We all are capable of impacting the ripple effect when we give our time, money, and/or abilities.

Paying it forward is so much fun!

Teaching Our Kids

As parents, we are not only teaching our kids the importance of handling their finances, but also the importance of giving. Even at their early ages, they are catching on.

Some would think it would be harder for kids to catch on to being great givers, however, we found their childlike innocence, open minds and giving hearts to be inspirational. So much so that we learned from them too. How could a child teach an adult to be better givers?

One example involved our 12-year-old daughter who illustrated her adaptability.

She had brought some of her spending money along to church one evening. Now mind you, our kids have their own charity, savings, and spending money from their weekly earnings. Out of their $6 allowance, $3 goes to savings, $2 goes to spending, and

$1 goes to charity. They're allowed to choose where they want to donate but the money designated to savings goes right to their savings accounts. They also have the option to earn money that usually goes into the envelope of their choice. Their spending money is theirs to use as long as it falls within our family value guidelines. Their charity money is for them to donate where they feel led to give.

When it came time for the offering, I saw Maggie with a crisp $10 bill from her spending envelope in her hand. Quite honestly, I wasn't sure why she had it out so I asked her. She looked at me with surprise and said, "What do you think?" and then said in a whisper it was for the offering. Do you know what my knee jerk reaction was? Instead of being happy or proud. I thought, "Oh, but that is $10 out of YOUR spending money. Don't you want to save it for something?"

I didn't say a thing, but raised my eyebrows instead. "Mom," she whispered, "I have more than enough spending money saved up at home. If I give this, then I will still have money left over." I asked her if she was sure she wanted to. "I want to give this," she replied. When the offering basket came around, she tossed in her $10 bill without hesitation. Leaning over to me with a smile she whispered in wonderment, "Mom, there are two checks in there, isn't that nice that people give?"

It hit me then how selfish I could be.

My immediate reaction was a closed fist "hang on to what you got so you can get more" attitude but my daughter saw where her money could serve a greater need.

She was right...she DID have more than "enough" — her feeling of contentment with what she had made me marvel at its simplicity. It certainly did make me smile as I thought, "You know what? We have more than enough too."

QUESTION TO PONDER:

How much is your "enough" in order for you to feel content?

Does the term "It's better to give then receive" ring true in your life? If not, what steps could you take to get there?

JEN'S GEMZ

Live With GRATITUDE!

As we express our gratitude, we must never forget that the highest appreciation is not to utter words, but to live by them.

~ John F. Kennedy

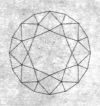

CHAPTER 14

Living Beyond Rich — Imagine Yourself There

> **Myth:** I am in a hopeless situation when it comes to getting out of debt.
>
> **Fact:** Taking intentional ACTION is key to success in finances.
>
> **Stat:** Countless people have gotten out of debt and YOU can too. ~ Jen McDonough

So how did the rest of our story go? Considering we were:

- The ones that didn't need a finance class, but were over $100,000 in debt.

- The ones who felt their overall financial troubles were only caused from ONE life event rather than a lifestyle choice.

- The ones who were completely stressed out and living in fear over their financial situation.

Well first off, our Robbie is doing great! We successfully completed and cash-flowed all 16 trips to Denver (~48 days away from work and home) for his medical research study. While Robbie continues to have Type I diabetes as of the writing of this book, we have faith that he contributed to helping find a cure.

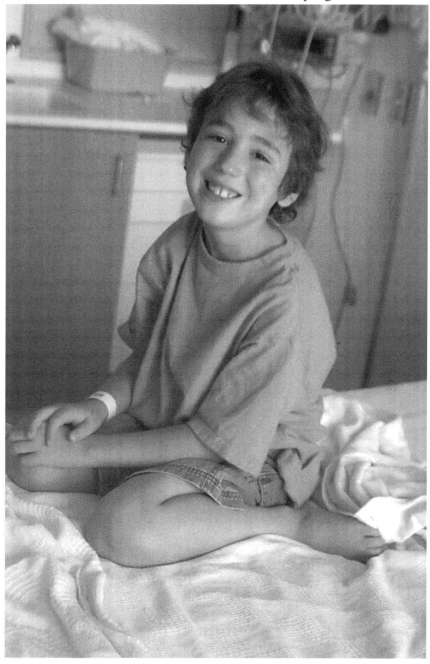

Our Results

What has this whole personal finance journey resulted in for our family?

I am proud to say that in three years, we have paid off over $150,000 worth of debt and paid cash for OVER $30,000 worth of medical related expenses. No government programs, no debt forgiveness programs, no debt consolidation programs... we did it by taking intentional ownership and action.

This was done on my wages as a secretary and Bob's salary while working in a customer representative service position as well as our part-time jobs.

In addition, we did this while being imperfect all along the way!

WHAT...not perfect?

> **JENSPIRATION**
>
> *We are ALL capable of achieving the impossible with faith, perseverance, and the willingness to take action on moving forward with a plan.*

Let me tell you, treating our failures as opportunities to learn how to win is one of our secrets to success. Whether it was the slip-ups we ourselves made or from unexpected events occurring, I can confidently tell you we never had one single perfect month. Yet even with all the blips along the way, we were able to transform into this awesome life we are living today.

In short, our world — one that was once filled with feelings of embarrassment, shame, fear, panic, and isolation has been

replaced by one complete with empowerment, peace, joy, gratitude, and freedom.

It is exhilarating looking back to see how something so awful was transformed into the richest experience of our lives.

Debt Is a Reality

Debt that once isolated us from the world now bonds us to the countless people that are struggling today.

If you yourself are in debt, know you are not alone.

Living up to your eyeballs in debt can be a reality for anyone no matter who you are, what you do for a living, how much you make, or what your life appears to be on the outside. Only by taking an honest inventory of where you stand can you see where you need to go.

If you are in are living with fear, stress, and/or panic about your finances, I am shouting to you right now:

- **"There IS hope, peace, and freedom within your reach. In order to gain that freedom, YOU are the one that has to make the choice to take intentional ownership and ACTION to make it happen."**

I would also tell you that when you get your finances in order, you will experience many of the same things we do each day, such as:

- **Enjoying peaceful slumbers instead of sleepless nights filled with anxiety, worry, and tension over finances.**

- **Living worry free, secure in knowing unexpected expenses such as car and house repairs will not drain your food money for the month — your emergencies are now inconveniences.**

- **Feeling the freedom of getting your mail and having no debt-related statements waiting for you.**

- Jumping to answer the phone, knowing it is a friend or relative on the other line and not a collection agency tracking you down for late payments

- Sensing the empowerment of not being stuck in a job you hate just because it pays the bills, but rather, having the flexibility to create and/or find the work you love.

- Relishing in a real a vacation and/or celebrating a holiday and not having the sinking feeling when the bills show up the next month.

- To be able to give generously and not wonder how on earth you'll be able to afford your own groceries.

- Experiencing the weight being lifted off your shoulders that you unknowingly carry today as each dollar of debt is eliminated.

JENSPIRATION

Eliminating debt affects families as a whole, not just your bank account.

For the parents out there, I want you to experience firsthand how incredibly rewarding it is to see your child(ren) transform right along with you. To watch them grow and:

- See them proudly pay for their own purchases rather than whine to you that they want something while you are at the store.

- To witness them become incredibly passionate givers with their own money rather than grabbing some change from you to toss in some charity bucket that they don't feel any connection to.

- To see their lives being shaped before your eyes as they comprehend that faith, perseverance, and taking action to a plan will lead them to being wealthy in all aspects in their lives, money being just one of them.

If you ask me if your journey will be easy, I have to honestly answer that no, it will most likely not be.

If you asked me if your journey will be worth it, I would take you by the shoulders, tell you to look at my eyes and firmly answer with a smile that "YES, IT IS MOST DEFINITELY WORTH IT."

I would also tell you that like us, you may experience lots of tears, laughter, bumps, scrapes, bruises, trauma, and drama while paying off debt; however, you WILL stand victoriously in the end.

I would advise you that your joyful times will be great; however it will be the trying times that make you stronger.

JENSPIRATION

While the road to Living Beyond Rich isn't always smooth, we can all find ways to get to our destination even when the road has twists and turns.

How empowering it is to know your pot of gold is within your reach?

Transformation From Ordinary to Extraordinary

We are a living example of how the ordinary can do the extraordinary...I know you can be too if you should choose!

There is no magic pill out there to make it happen, rather it is a choice of action we all must do for own ourselves.

My sincere hope is that you will decide that your life is worth Living Beyond Rich and that you will take intentional steps to start your journey of freedom and transformation today.

Remember, your journey will be a marathon, not a sprint. Any marathon in life worth doing will need to start with taking that first courageous step.

While your marathon course may seem long and difficult at times, I promise you the journey will be worth the effort!

My best advice (said with a smile of course) for taking charge of your financial future is summed up in these few words:

1. Decide to go for it and then;

2. **MOVE IT!** Remember, the key to success starts with ABC (Action Brings change).

Lastly, remember the life you live today will be the life you experience tomorrow.

Many blessings!

Live Beyond Rich. Live Beyond Awesome.

~ Jen McDonough
Motivational Storyteller, Coach & Author of *Living Beyond Rich & Living Beyond Awesome*
Mom to four AWESOME kids & wife to one AWESOME husband

JEN'S GEMZ

Live With RICHNESS!

There are people who have money and people who are rich.

~ *Coco Chanel*

CHAPTER 15

Your Starting Line to Living Beyond Rich

Myth: Getting out of debt can only be for the ones who are already rich.

Fact: We ALL have a CHOICE to taking action to Live Beyond Rich.

Stat: "Contrary to popular belief, frugality is the foundation of wealth. Mundane consumption habits that are void of luxury-car purchases and fabulous yachting sprees may not impress the neighbors or the media, but then, impressing the public isn't the goal of most first-generation millionaires. Financial independence is." — The Millionaire Next Door 1996

In my role as a motivational storyteller, author, and freedom debt elimination coach. I find such joy and passion in sharing our story in order to give hope and inspiration to others.

My intentional purpose is for people to discover that they too CAN experience an extraordinary life.

If you are waiting to transform your financial lives...here is a message just for you:

"You CAN do this! Just smile and GET MOVING!"

My life has been filled with inspiring mentors along the way. In paying it forward, I would be delighted to be considered one of your mentors as well. Join our movement of encouraging ordinary people to do extraordinary things such as eliminating debt by connecting with me through my blogs, newsletters, and/or podcasts at http://www.TheIronJen.com.

In not wanting the story to end, I leave you with an inspirational story of an incredible person who is starting their own freedom finance journey. Her story was much like ours when we started in that living without debt seemed to be out of reach.

After reading her story, I want to challenge you the reader with this one important question...When does your freedom finance journey begin?

Remember, I believe in you. If I can do it, YOU can do it!

~ Jen McDonough "The Iron Jen"

My Freedom Finance Journey Starting Line Has Begun...

~ Kathleen Crandall

I've had many wake-up calls in my life but none delivered as powerful a blow as the day I realized I had $3.25 left to my name. I had a choice: invest it in a gallon of gas or blow it on a gallon of milk. But, like everyone, there is more to the story. And everyone has a story...

Kathy's Story

The year 2000 marked the start to my terrible, horrible, no good, very bad decade of life lessons. I had just ended a tumultuous two-year divorce and custody battle that ripped apart hearts, hopes, and dreams and left me with the most precious gifts of all — full custody of my two-year old son and four-year old daughter and a blind cocker spaniel. It cost me every penny I had saved and invested and the PR firm I had built over the past decade and left me with $50,000 in legal fees and $50,000 of marital debt. I was broke but eternally optimistic that all would be well.

I took a job as senior vice president for a very big international PR firm and built a healthcare division with a $4 million portfolio of business. My nose to the grindstone, I put in 12–14 billable hours a day in the office and at home while I juggled being a devoted mother and diligent homeowner.

Two years from the day I was granted the divorce and custody I paid off the divorce lawyers. That same day I was diagnosed with two inoperable brain tumors. Two steps forward, five steps back.

The next six months was spent in and out of MRIs, doctor's offices and researching my options on the internet. I was told my chances of surviving invasive surgery was 50:50 by one neurosurgeon while another recommended we just wait and see as the tumors grew. I finally landed at Mayo Clinic for a life-saving procedure that the other surgeons weren't trained to perform. I learned to be my own advocate and it saved my life.

Along this path to restoring my health I lost my job and my house and incurred another $50,000 in legal fees as a result of trying to leave the campsite cleaner than when I got there. I won a battle and lost the war.

Four years after I was granted the divorce, I sold everything we owned and moved my little family from our 4,000 square foot dream house to a 750 square foot rental on the other side of town. Desperate, I took a job making ¾ less than my former salary and lived paycheck to paycheck for the next year wondering how on earth I got to this. I used credit cards to make ends meet until they reached their max and they closed my accounts.

Pivotal Day

One sunny day I woke up and realized I had $3.25 to my name. On this sunny day full of possibilities we also ran out of milk.

This was my day of judgment and reckoning and I had a choice: Do I buy the gallon of milk to save face with my children who wondered why Mommy didn't have milk for their cereal or do I put that $3.25 into a gallon of gas to get me to a meeting that might net me a client and relaunch my PR firm?

I bought the gallon of gas. And I landed the client.

Over the next three years I clawed my way back to breaking even. And in 2007, seven years and six months from my divorce date, I was able to buy our "just right" house and felt the ground beneath me shake a little less.

Debt is Normal Right?

Somehow I believed that being more than $100,000 in debt was normal. I believed that I was living like everyone else and that it was normal to have a car payment and credit cards and lines of credit to live the American dream. I resigned myself to the fact that I'd never be able to be debt free and that the minimum monthly payments were to be a permanent line item in my budget. I made up for all we had to give up and go without the past eight years with frequent trips to Costco and Target filling bags with stuff we didn't need. And I thought it was okay because none of what we had was "luxury," or ostentatious. We simply had the basics.

I thought I was being responsible because I had a "budget" and while the income ebbed and flowed, I was diligent about looking at my line item budget. And yet, despite making more money than ever before and paying cash for everything, I was still struggling. Where on earth was the money going?

Financial Freedom Plan Begins

Then I met Jen. I learned about her Total Money Makeover story and how she and her husband tackled $100,000 of debt in a few years. I proudly showed her my budget and forecast anticipating how impressed she would be with my financial aptitude. She oooed and ahhhed at my elaborate Excel documents and then asked very gently, "But how do you know how much you are actually spending?"

And with that, the course of my life took a hard right down the right road.

Yes, I had a budget, but I had no record of what I actually spent. I used QuickBooks® and Money® software but because I used cash (without tracking the spending) and was sloppy about how I categorized each expense, I never really knew where it went.

Jen gave me the gift of a subscription to Dave Ramsay's Total Money Makeover online. Within 24 hours of playing with the tool and altering my fabulous Excel document, I learned that I actually spent, on average, $1,200 a month in groceries and household "necessities," not the $500 I had "budgeted." In fact, I actually spent three times the amount budgeted for every variable expense and more. There it was in black and white. I had very little to show for the money that slipped through my fingers.

For the first time in my life, I started to engage with my money. I tracked every little expense and I went back and totaled what I had actually spent (and paid off) in the past so I could feel a sense of what I did accomplish.

I got control of mindless and emotional spending that held me captive in debt. I vowed to never again put my head in the

sand when it came to money. I shifted my belief from "money is evil" to "I earned it and it is in my control to live in abundance."

I became thoughtful and intentional in my spending and tracking every single expense. I found it surprisingly easy to not spend needlessly. I became very gazelle-like in my dodging and weaving around the obstacles in my mind and distractions in my schedule to reach my goal of staying on a budget. I learned to say no. I was motivated by saving dollars and putting it against debt. I printed out my fabulous Excel document and taped it to my wall so I can visualize every line item. I can see the diminishing blue lines of debt snowballing from month to month and the increasing green lines of savings in my emergency fund, college and retirement accounts.

Where I Am Today and Where I Will Be Tomorrow

I am intensely focused on my goals and nothing will get in my way. I still love my Excel document and the discipline of using this and the Total Money Makeover online tool — both have brought clarity to how and why I spend. I have reengaged with my money and no longer live in fear or shame and, while I still have a ways to go, I have hope.

I have reached my goal of a $1,000 emergency fund and will be completely debt free by April 2014. I will have my mortgage paid off in September 2019 — a 30-year fixed mortgage paid off in 12 years and three months. A savings in interest of $154,513.11.

This is more than just a game of eliminating a decade of debt in two years. This is about changing my entire belief system. I no longer believe that it is normal to have debt. I no longer buy into the American Dream being built on credit cards, lines of credit and borrowing to get what you want or need. I no longer believe that when bad things happen to good people it is okay make people believe everything's okay with the illusion of borrowed abundance.

I believe having a plan and a vision is crucial. Bad things happen to all of us. It's how we handle the misfortunes that make us a success story. And we can't and shouldn't go it alone.

Every mountain climber who reaches the rare air had a Sherpa at their side to help carry the load.

Along my journey I've learned the lessons of humility, patience, faith and how the love of family and friends will lift you to believe that dreams come true. Because they do.

Advice:

- Set your goals and ask for help to bring them to life.

- Be intentional and thoughtful with every action.

- Say please and thank you.

- Tell your truth and pull back the curtain.

- Be weird by being intentional with your money because keeping up with the Joneses is exhausting and fruitless.

Peace,

~ Kathleen Crandall

Single mother of two teenagers, two cats, and a dog.

Living the dream as a Personal Branding Coach and owner of a PR firm. Debt free in April 2014.

Mortgage free in September 2019.

Retirement fully funded by age 62.

FINAL QUESTIONS FROM JEN TO PONDER:

Do you have empowerment, peace, and joy over your finances?

If not, are you ready to become intentional and choose your pivotal date of transformation?

Where will you be tomorrow? In the next 5 years? In the next 10 years? In the next 20 years?

If you don't start today, what makes you think tomorrow will be any different?

Are you ready to starting Living Beyond Rich? If so my friends, I will look forward to seeing you at the top!

PART V
Awesome Expert Advice

JEN'S GEMZ

Live With Action!

People are always blaming their circumstances for what they are. I don't believe in circumstances. The people who get on in this world are the people who get up and look for the circumstances they want, and if they can't find them, make them.

~ George Bernard Shaw

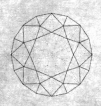

CHAPTER 16

Gaining Financial Control is Empowering!

AWESOME EXPERT ADVICE

by Jackie Walters

Guest Author & Expert Jackie Walters Shares Financial Wisdom:

Nothing brings a smile to my face and warms my heart more than when someone tells me they just paid off a debt or saved 50% at the grocery store by using coupons. My gift is to teach people how to use money responsibly so that they are not burdened and they can be blessed and give back to our world.

I'm married with two children and had been in and out of debt for years. I did not always know how to manage money or resist the temptations of over spending. In fact I am embarrassed at how I spent money when I was younger.

I went through Dave Ramsey's Financial Peace University (FPU) several years ago, before paying off debt was cool. Dave's lessons and techniques went on to bless my family and inspire me to become the financial expert I am today.

Soon after I completed Dave's course, the economy took a dive. Although we had just paid off most of our debt, we were living with little cushion or room for error when our own pay cuts started. We made the decision to take what we had learned and put it to good use. We buckled down as a family in order to change our behavior and support our collective goals.

We knew that, according to The Wall Street Journal, 70% of Americans live paycheck to paycheck. That meant that 7 out of 10 of our neighbors were only one paycheck away from disaster. As we looked around our neighborhood, it saddened me to see homes going up for foreclosure. Even with our decreased income, I could see how our family was benefiting from the behaviors we learned.

Through this experience, I knew I had to be the messenger of hope as God had placed a passion in my heart to help make a difference in people's lives.

I felt a tug on my heart and an invisible tap on my shoulder when our church decided to provide Financial Peace University to our congregation. I quickly volunteered and was appointed director of the program. This was no easy undertaking to a congregation with over 12,000 weekly attendees. I was humbled but motivated as so many people were struggling — I wanted them to have the same hope and motivation we had. Many did not know how to plan, how to save, how to cut back, or how to use money in God's way.

I trained 75+ coordinators to lead 577 people through Financial Peace University.

Out of those 577 ordinary everyday people, we were saddened to see the total debt that burdened our friends and neighbors. Our group of 577 participants collectively owed over $10 million dollars in non-mortgage debt.

The pain and pressure that these ordinary people were experiencing was enormous. Although I could imagine the stress in the marriages, I could also sense the relief and hope that was coming. Throughout our eight-week series, it was a joy to watch as the groups shared with each other with compassion and understanding.

I am proud to report that in just eight weeks this group of 577 people went on to collectively pay off $2 million in personal debt!

Yes, 20% of their debt vanished in ONLY 2 months! Through the course, they were given the tools, motivation, and fellowship they needed to change their behavior.

When meeting with clients today, my message is that getting one's finances in order is not a quick fix or a get-rich-quick scheme. It's a challenging first step to becoming wealthy that requires diligent, hard work. However, the results are life altering.

The result of getting one's finances in order is that families stay together. Stress is reduced, and joy comes to those who have struggled their way to the top. Their views on money and life are altered and they are not afraid to be different in order to succeed.

I have heard and witnessed firsthand countless stories of mountains of debt that snuck up on good hearted people. Debt tried to destroy each one of them. I have also witnessed mountains of debt slowly crumble and melt away once people have the tools, hope, and support.

It was truly amazing to see peace and empowerment descend on people when they take personal accountability to lift the heavy burdens caused from their own financial actions.

One of the reasons for Financial Peace University's success is the focus placed on the families, not just the individuals. One thing I know my family learned is that communicating about money is important. Once we learned to talk about it, then managing our spending behavior became easier. We learned that personal finance is 80% behavior and 20% knowledge. This is why support, especially family support, is so critical. Without it, it's an uphill battle, herding cats, all the way. Families that go through Financial Peace University will see the end result and that is financial peace.

Coordinating and facilitating Financial Peace University was a very humbling and exciting experience. Having the courage to step up as a Financial Peace University leader allowed me to be an instrument to inspire change within people. I found that I grew more passionate and knowledgeable along with the people in their journeys and changed just as much.

The experience also has served me in my current role of a financial coach to others that are struggling. Not only have I seen lives changed, but I have met some amazing people with some extraordinary stories.

If you are ready to start your own journey, know that peace, prosperity, and freedom are within your reach.

Jackie Walters: Founder of The Budget Works (http://the-budgetworks.com). She specializes in personal financial coaching and keeps herself plugged into this growing community. Jackie is very passionate about helping others succeed financially and shares her deep knowledge on a regular basis. Jackie believes that the key to responsible personal finance is managing a budget. She emphasizes that using a budget can help to control spending and uncover ways to save. You can follow Jackie on Twitter @TheBudgetWorks or on Facebook at The Budget Works.

CHAPTER 17

~~~~~~~~~~~~~~~

Single Mom's Gaining Financial Independence

AWESOME EXPERT ADVICE

Single Mom's Gaining Financial Independence

By Jennifer Finnegan

Guest Author & Expert Jennifer Finnegan Shares Financial Wisdom:

In the fall of 2005 I suddenly found myself to be a single mom. I had a car that was paid off, two children – ages one and three, and I had no clue what to do! I found myself in instant poverty; I was in need of a job outside the home, and a helping hand from the government. Fast forwarding six years, God used my pain of becoming a single mom to grow an organization that helps single moms.

I now have the privilege of hearing hundreds of stories from single moms each year that have been divorced, never married, or widowed. Many of them, like myself, have had to learn to re invent their lives, including their financial lives. Perhaps, like some of us, you have found yourself suddenly a single mom and are asking the question, how am I going to make it?

To begin with we are not alone. Many single moms have gone before us and are thriving today because of positive choices they made early on in their journeys.

In my own beginning I felt overwhelmed with the emotional upheaval of being abandoned by my husband, caring for my children alone, and figuring out how to financially sustain.

After a month of sitting in the muck I prayed and asked the Lord to show me what to do. About a week later I was moved to do an assessment of my needs, my children's needs, and our needs as a new three person family. I laid out how many hours I felt I needed to be present with my kids, how often I needed "me" time, how much household responsibility I could handle on my own, where we needed to live, and many other things.

Today I encourage every single mom to start with a needs assessment. Write it out, draw pictures, make a chart, form it in a way that speaks to you. From this assessment you can then begin to see the bigger picture and start finding the pieces needed to meet the needs identified. Some common needs that must be met on the onset of becoming a single mom are our family's basic, emotional, and financial needs.

Many times single moms like myself need government help to provide medical insurance, food, cash, and/or other resources. If you are struggling in any of these areas you may contact your local agency to begin working with a case worker. It is normal for most single moms to receive assistance for a season while they are getting back on their feet.

A few weeks ago a woman came into my office after three years of being a single mom. She was struggling to pay her rent while she worked, went to school, and cared for her two children. After looking through her finances I asked her why she was not accepting food assistance. She proceeded to share that she felt like others would look down on her for taking government aid.

This is an all too common statement and one that has lead many single moms into debt.

Government aid can be a helping hand to help you restart and move on to a sustainable future. If this is a concern you are battling with I would encourage you to talk to a case worker or financial advisor on how you can incorporate government assistance into a financial plan that will lead you out of poverty. Remember there are many seasons to come in your future and there will come a time when you will be able to give back in some way and encourage a new single mom or dad.

Many single moms today tend to be operating from an old financial budget that was used before becoming a single mom and that needs to change. Whether you have gone from a two person income to a one person income or from a one person income to now incorporating a child into the budget it is essential to create a new budget that will work for you and your family. Perhaps this is the first time you have been in charge of your finances. It can seem overwhelming at first but like many new things breaking it down into manageable goals will help.

To begin find a budget plan that will work for you. I prefer the envelope system. It allows me to see my weekly financial allotments, it gives me opportunity to impart budgeting to my kids as they look to see if we have the finances in our entertainment slot to go out to eat, and it allows me to incorporate a wonderful reward at the end of the week if we maintained our budget.

I struggled to be self-controlled in the area of finances shortly after I became a single mom and I needed a way to allow myself to splurge in a controlled way. Two years into my new life I began to set splurge "goals" along with my financial goals. For example, we had a great coffee shop in town and if I kept my budget for the week on Sunday morning I would treat myself to a latte and my kids to hot chocolate. Kids love reaching the reward and it can be a great way to teach them financial principles and self control.

One of the crucial elements of any budget is having an understanding and awareness of your housing costs. Once they become single moms many women can no longer afford the house they are living in. It may be hard to make the decision to move to more affordable housing early on but it is crucial. If you are in a home you cannot afford for two, ten, or eighteen months you will deplete any additional savings you may have and/or go into debt.

In the beginning of my own journey, I quickly realized that acquiring a house would also be acquiring all the upkeep of the house. I found it beneficial to rent so that the responsibility of upkeep was not fully on my shoulders.

Another housing option is to share a house with another single mom family. A single mom in our organization currently rents a room for her and her newborn at a low rate in exchange for caring for the other single mom's daughter. This housing choice is not always available but the more we interact with other single moms and find out what their needs are the more we can experience support and networking.

Another point to assess in creating a new budget is our income potentials. There may be a sixty thousand a year job available but it requires weekend traveling. If one of your needs is to be home with your children and this new job would conflict with that need I believe it is best to find a lower paying job and recreate your budget than to go against a valid need you and/or your family has. This can be tough.

I remember turning down a full time job early on because I felt the need to transition slowly from my being at home all the time with my children to becoming a full-time working mom. I felt discouraged at the time for not being able to financially afford more for my family. Looking back today I am so grateful for the slow transition — by turning down the higher paying job and accepting a job that fit with our needs I was able to create a safe and secure home for my children to heal in and begin to flourish in.

Some common mistakes many of us make as single moms:

- Relying on child support in our budgets even if it has proven to be inconsistent.

- Competing financially with our ex-spouses.

- Purchasing material items out of guilt we may feel in regards to what our child(ren) have gone through.

- Purchasing material items as a band aid to cover up our own pain.

Many of the poor financial decisions we make in the short time following becoming a single mom is out of the emotional pain we are experiencing. I have found that having a counselor to talk to, seek advice from, and be held accountable to is a great way to offset the lack of another parent's support in the home.

We are not alone as single moms. There is a vast community of other single moms seeking to live life well. The gifts of love, faith, and Godliness that we can give to our children are the richest inheritance they could ever have.

Blessings on your journey as a single parent.

Jennifer Finnegan: Jennifer is an advocate for living life well as a single mom, which she has been for 7 years — a life not only viable, but flourishing. It was out of this passion for creating supportive community that Jennifer founded Single MOMM in October of 2008. Her desire is to build a support system unique to the area that empowers other single moms to go from surviving, to thriving.

Jennifer is also a regional speaker. She uses storytelling to bring a realness and fullness to the stage, inviting others into her life and helping to inspire, encourage, and bring hope.

Jennifer lives in Traverse City. She is passionate about being grateful for the present, and she spends her free time seeking adventures with her two fantastic children.

http://www.singlemomm.org/

CHAPTER 18

~~~~~~~~~~

Attention Young Adults! Don't Follow Our Lead (We've purchased our way into slavery)

AWESOME EXPERT ADVICE

by Glen Steinson

Guest Author & Expert Glen Steinson Shares Financial Wisdom:

When we think about inventions that have both a positive and negative impact on our society, many come to mind.

Explosives have been used to blast roadways through mountains and also mine minerals deep underground. Yet, this same tool can be intentionally used to kill and destroy.

Similarly, modern inventions like the internet can be used to bring societies together, facilitate trade and share knowledge freely. But when used in an uncontrolled and self-destructive manner, online habits can form that devastate the individual and tear family units apart.

I believe there is something else in our society that can be used properly and yet is abused so frequently that it threatens to permanently cripple every man, woman and child living in the developed world.

No, I'm not talking about nuclear or biological devices — I'm talking about revolving credit.

Yes, you heard that right. Credit cards and lines of credit pose a far greater risk to our future well-being than terrorism, addictions and divorce <u>combined</u>. This invention has caused far more problems than the benefits it claims to offer. Ask almost anyone ages 31 to 45 if they've taken on additional debt over the past decade and, if they fall into the statistical majority (and are honest), they'll respond "Yes."

Parents used to teach their kids that you didn't buy anything unless you had saved up and could pay for it in cash. Nowadays, Mom and Dad are demonstrating that you can have anything you want — right now.

Why wait when you can charge it?

Get it today and pay for it later.

Easy monthly payments take our dreams and make them reality. Or do they?

Attention Young Adults — I Am Talking To You:

As the leaders of the next generation, you've already proven that you're ambitious, self-motivated and able to assess the long-term outcome of your decisions. As you advance into your career, possibly get married, start a family and make major purchase decisions — you should observe recent history so you can rise above it. In order to live life to its fullest and truly enjoy the fruit of your labor, let's take a few moments to study the financial landscape. Is credit going to help you achieve your goals or is it going to deceive you into a false sense of security?

Wow! What just happened?

Let's hit the numbers briefly.

If you earn $40k a year and have a total of $20k in outstanding debt, your debt-to-income ratio is 50%. That's easy to understand.

It's also easy to understand that, with a little budgeting and some lump sum payments, that debt can be paid down to $0 in a relatively short time. Whatever the debt is (student loans, vehicle payments, or that spring break trip to Cancun), once it's paid off, the money that you would have been giving to the lender now stays in your pocket. You're no longer obligated to them. You have been released from that claim on your hard-earned money. You are no longer a slave to the lender!

But the numbers for those ages 31 to 45 are a bit higher. The past decade has yielded rock bottom interest rates in an attempt to fuel the economy and get people spending on big ticket items. And you know what? It worked.

In fact, the strategy worked so well that the debt-to- income ratio climbed past 75% and hit an even 100%. For every dollar of household income earned, an equal dollar was owed to a creditor — a creditor that at one time looked like the best answer to a financial challenge.

Want an addition on the house? Call the banker.

Have some major vehicle repairs? Grab your Visa.

Weekend skiing trip to Aspen with friends? Take an advance from the new line of credit.

This behavior of immediate gratification didn't stop when the debt ratio reached 100%. It continued to grow. The generation ahead of you has allowed their ratio to creep up to 150%. Ouch! This frivolous use of someone else's money was done under the assumption that the income would always be there to make the payments. It has also been justified because the payments are "manageable." (On a side note: what happens when interest rates move up a mere 5%? If you owe $60k, that adds another $250 a month to your payments. Again I say "Ouch!")

Millennials to the Rescue!

As a member of Generation Y, you have a unique and time-sensitive opportunity to step out from under the mind-numbing influence that revolving credit has had on your parents. To help you, here is a very simple concept to remember;

If you consistently spend more than you make — you <u>will</u> become a slave to your creditors.

If you consistently spend less than you make — you will enjoy freedom.

Sounds foolish and a little cliché? Jump ahead 10 years and imagine yourself in the typical household burdened with debt. You've just received notice from your employer that the company you work for is downsizing and, although you'll still have a job, your hours have been cut in half. When the credit card statements show up in the mail, how does your bondage feel now?

We've watched in amazement as your generation has advanced at a far faster pace than any generation previous to it. Your desire to learn and succeed in life is unwavering and holds with it the power to break the preconceived plans the banks and finance companies have for your future. Don't let them draw you into their snare with easy credit and years of payments on things you can't even remember anymore.

The phrase "Living Beyond Rich" includes so much more than just money. But how you approach money — our relation-

ship with it and the prudent use of it — directly determines whether you have control of it or if it will control you. Whose account do you want your income to go into? Yours? Or the Bank?

Glen Steinson: Your host on the **Stewardship Weekly** podcast. Passionate about being good stewards of all that has been entrusted to our care, Glen shares his thoughts and convictions as they pertain to our **Income** and **Assets, Time** and **Talents.** Always ready to share with others in person, Glen has an active speaking ministry in southern Ontario, Canada. Be sure to visit http:// www.StewardshipWeekly.com and let him know that you've read this book! He WILL respond to you personally.

CHAPTER 19

~~~~~~

Pay Attention Not Interest

AWESOME EXPERT ADVICE

by Steve Stewart

Guest Author & Expert Steve Stewart Shares Financial Wisdom:

What if I told you the secret to becoming wealthy was no secret at all? Would you believe me? And what if I told you that you already knew the secret?

The secret to becoming wealthy is simply this: Live on less than you make and do something smart with the difference. Yep. You knew that already, didn't you? Yeah, I thought I did too until it finally dawned on me that I wasn't following the "do something smart with the difference" part.

You see, a millionaire is not typically the one who wins the lottery or gets a large signing bonus. In fact, a majority of lottery winners and sports professionals are broke in only a few years after "hitting the big one." Why? Consumerism.

Consumerism has taken this country by the wallets. Marketing is at an all-time high with more advertisements per square mile than people. Okay, I made that statistic up but you probably considered it to be true to some degree, didn't you? Walk outside of your workplace and you will probably see powerful examples of branding or advertisement. How big is the emblem on the cars? How many billboards can you hit with a rock from the very spot you are standing (provided you are reading this outside)? Have you counted the number of commercials that are squeezed between each segment of your favorite reality TV show?

How can we resist? Anything we want is ours for the taking. All we need is to slide a piece of plastic across the counter and that new gadget/tool/purse is ours! Life is great, for now. Unfortunately, this behavior is hazardous to our wealth.

We spend what we have today without seriously taking into consideration tomorrow. Our retirement accounts are proof of that. Reports have shown us that a majority of baby boomers have less than $50,000 saved for their golden years. More and more households are being affected by higher prices of groceries and gasoline. Student loan debt has reached dangerous levels and is going to destroy the futures of those who thought they were entitled to a good education. The future is bleak for those who didn't plan far enough ahead to be prepared for life.

How can someone learn to live on less than they make? The simple answer is to live on a budget. A budget will tell you in a matter of minutes how much it takes to exist and how much you need for other obligations (debt). Anything left over can be used for short-term or long-term savings.

Our family started living on a budget in 2004 and decided to pay for things without debt. Every month we decide where our money should go, make adjustments during the month when unexpected things happen, but always spend/save down to zero. Once we were out of debt we were able to remodel our kitchen, take nice family vacations in the summer, and are putting money away for the future. We aren't millionaires but many would call us wealthy.

Why am I telling you this? It is because I know for a fact that I'm the type of guy who would swipe a credit card with the full intention of paying the balance off next month, forgetting that there already was a balance that wasn't paid off the month before because I "needed" more gadgets. That's a dangerous situation that most Americans believe they can handle, and most Americans are broke.

The great news is that if I can do it, you can do it too! No signing bonus, no lottery jackpot, just forecasting expenses and deciding to stick to the money plan.

I can't tell you that living on less than you make is easy to do, but it isn't complicated. Regardless of what the billboards are trying to say, buying things we need and saving for things we want will make our lives much happier over the long haul — much better than the instant gratification of stuff we purchased with debt. I know this to be true because now we are paying attention, not interest.

Steve Stewart: Resides with this wife in St. Louis, MO where they have been raising their daughter for over a decade. He is a Personal Finance Architect helping everyday Americans build a solid foundation on which to design their house of financial freedom and is the only independent Financial Coach to be featured in a segment of the Dave Ramsey Show. His passion is helping people pay attention, not interest. You can find more great articles, downloadable audio lessons, and video blogs on his website, http://www.moneyplansos.com/

CHAPTER 20

Keys to Finding Income

AWESOME EXPERT ADVICE

by Jeff Pattison

Guest Author & Expert Jeff Pattison Shares Financial Wisdom:

As an HR professional, all too often, I see how personal finance problems affect people in their careers and happiness at work. This bleeds into their ability to do a good job, either because of the poor attitude they bring to work (worried, complaining, unenthused, or stressed out) or their ability to be at work on time and consistently. It happens to good people who feel like they just can't get a break. The car breaking down or the baby-sitter being sick are two common examples.

Without any cushion in their money situation, it can't help but affect them at work— which only makes things worse! They are also more likely to stay in a job they don't really like because "it's something that pays the bills".

But on occasion, I get to witness how someone has taken a tough situation and not only resolved it, but actually made their long-term career much better in the process.

I've found that there is one key trait in every one of these winners. It's their decision to become extremely PROACTIVE in their willingness to better themselves.

In the best-selling book *"The Seven Habits of Highly Effective People"* by Stephen R. Covey, the first habit is "Be Proactive." It is the decision to take initiative in life by realizing that your decisions are the primary determining factor for effectiveness in your life.

To me, there are three aspects of taking control of your career and your money. I call it the "APP for Success". In this case, the APP is an acronym for Attitude, Passion and Planning.

1. **Attitude** — It's no surprise that anyone who chooses to overcome any obstacle, including money and career problems, must start with having the right attitude. This begins with the way you view yourself and the way you treat others. Without the right attitude, everything else breaks down. When things get extra tough, people without a positive attitude tend to give up or rub others the wrong way. **Book suggestion:** *The Power of Positive Thinking* **by Norman Vincent Peale.**

2. **Passion** — It shouldn't shock anyone to find that those who make the biggest strides in their careers (and ultimately, their money) are doing things that they enjoy. We've got to take some time to be introspective and figure out what it is that we enjoy and get to doing it in some way or another. Starting out, that doesn't mean we have to know the exact job we want, but we should know our own personality and what that says about the general type of work we should be doing. Do more of what interests you. **Suggestion: Ask your friends and family what they think you are passionate about and are especially good at. You may be surprised what they can tell you that you have a hard time seeing yourself.**

3. **Planning** — We can have all the right attitude and passion, but without having a plan in place to do something, it won't happen. I've met a lot of wonderful people with great attitudes who really know themselves well, but are unwilling to sit down and create a plan they can follow to make the change they need. This is where having a willingness to be proactive really pays off. **Suggestion: Contact me at my website and I will gladly provide you with a career planning worksheet and tips for making the changes you want and need to your current job and career situation.**

Short-term options:

When it comes to making money, the short-term is what one needs to focus on right now to get over financial hurdles. This is where folks can roll up their sleeves for a short period and do things no normal person would want to do. Interestingly, this affects the long-term, which is ultimately where the real impact is made.

For those in this position, the best choice is to get an idea of what your passions are and find a way to help others using that. As an example, maybe you love to work in the yard. There are plenty of opportunities to mow yards, do landscaping, etc. This type of thing can be done around your normal schedule which is a major advantage. You just have to get started!

Spread the word with people you know. If you are on Facebook, mention it there. Something like — "Hey everyone. With my love for landscaping, I'm looking to find others who feel just the opposite and would like some help. Let me know if you know anyone I can provide a service to. I would appreciate if you could share this with your friends." It's a start and it doesn't cost a thing.

If you aren't sure about that just yet, consider finding a more traditional option that fits your need to just make some extra cash. Someone with a great attitude, willingness to work, and readiness to be bold in letting people know they are interested will go a long ways to bringing in extra income.

This may not be the dream job, but it is filling a necessary gap that will allow you to excel later. Again, ask around and keep your eyes open. If possible, make sure this is a job that is close to home. It's tough to take on a second job. Don't make it tougher by giving yourself additional hurdles to deal with.

Long-term:

I am always interested in seeing how folks who have made the tough decision to become extremely proactive about their finances as they tend to end up changing the direction of their careers. For way too long, they've been laboring through work each week, doing what they had to do to get by. Now when they become financially free, they become some of the best employees. You know what happens to the best employee's right? They end up with more opportunities. More opportunities create more ability to choose what YOU want to do with your career.

There is no such thing as getting lucky in your career or with your money. It is a pattern of decisions, starting in the short-term, that gets the ball rolling. The sooner you decide to succeed, decide to figure out your real strengths and interests, and make a plan to do it, the sooner you can live the life you want, both inside and outside of work. GET PROACTIVE and see the results!

Jeff Pattison: Speaker and Human Resources professional from St. Louis, MO with 15 years of experience in the areas of interviewing, hiring, coaching, training, and employee development. To learn more about Jeff and to follow his blog, visit http://www.jeffpattison.com. Also, feel free to connect at twitter (@pattisonjeff) or on LinkedIn.

CHAPTER 21

Budgeting Basics

AWESOME EXPERT ADVICE

by Ashley Barnett

Guest Author & Expert Ashley Barnett Shares
Financial Wisdom:

The financial process can seem overwhelming when you are first starting out. You've been busy living your life doing all the stuff you've been told you "should" do. You got a good job, bought a house, had a few kids, financed a few cars and then one day you wake up and realize your finances aren't what they could be. You realize that if you don't make a change you might be working forever. But where do you start? How do you ask for help when doing so probably means admitting that things aren't going as well as you've been thinking? Besides, who should you even ask?

Everyone you know is in the same boat as you!

The financial process isn't as complicated as the finance industry wants you to believe. It's actually pretty simple. Unfortunately, the industry can't tell you that or you would stop buying all their expensive products. So they muck it up with a lot of fancy terms and play on your fears to keep you coming to them for their "solutions."

The end goal of any financial plan is to retire, the sooner the better. You get to retire when your savings or passive income (the money you make without working) is enough for you to live on for the rest of your life. That is what they call "financial independence."

I know what you're thinking. "Financial independence! Let's get real, I just need to know how to juggle all these bills!" I know, it seems like a lofty goal, but we'll get there. I promise.

The bedrock of all things financial is the budget. Having a budget will help control spending. Don't freak; it's just a guide that will make sure that you are spending your money where it's important to you. You make the budget ... not me ... not some online calculator ... you. It's your money and you get to decide where to spend it. There are two important elements of budgeting — creating the budget and living on the budget.

Creating the Budget

Ideally, your budget will start at the beginning of each month. It's also perfectly fine to budget for each paycheck before the check arrives. Before the start of your budgeting period write down the income you expect to receive. If your income isn't regular estimate on the low side of what you expect. Then write down all the bills that will be due during the timeframe with which you are working. Don't forget items for which you want to start saving up. For example, if your car is going to need new tags next month you might want to start socking away a few dollars now to ease the burden when that comes around.

Also, don't forget the fun stuff. Remember this is your budget. What do you want to spend money on? You can't spend more than you have coming in but try to fit something special in there for yourself.

Living on the Budget

So you got your budget all set up and ready to guide your spending choices for the next few weeks. Great! Now it's time to make sure reality lines up with what you planned. Tracking your spending is the second half of budgeting. Find a system that works for you. Personally, I keep my receipts from the day and enter my spending into the budget each evening. The important part is to track your spending every day to keep it from getting away from you.

If you find that you are going over budget in a category, you can cut from someplace else to stay on track. The first time you budget this will happen quite a bit. That's okay. It doesn't mean the budget isn't working. Just keep making adjustments as you go and over time the process will get smoother. Just stick with it!

I'm willing to bet just tracking your spending against your budget caused you to make some changes. You might already have some money in savings! That's awesome. Once you have the budget working you can move on to tackling your debt.

Debt Elimination

List all the debts you have including the balance, the interest rate, and the payment. The payoff plan goes like this; pick one debt and throw every extra dollar towards it that you can while making the minimum payment on all the others. When that debt is paid off you move on to the next and the next and the next until all the debt is gone. Tackle each debt with vengeance until each one is gone.

Phew! You did it! You are debt free and on the road to financial independence. Congratulations!

Next steps…gaining wealth through investing.

Ashley Barnett: Ashley spends her days helping people control their money and get out of debt. As a personal finance coach she believes that tracking one's spending and getting out of debt are the keys to wealth. You can also find her writing the personal finance blog, http://moneytalkscoaching.com/, and on twitter at @MoneyTalksCoach

CHAPTER 22

~~~~~~~~~~~~~~

How to Put Together the First Budget

AWESOME EXPERT ADVICE

by Matt Wegner

Guest Author & Expert Matt Wegner Shares Financial Wisdom:

Your first budget can be very intimidating. If you've never attempted one before, it's often overwhelming just figuring out where to start. But it doesn't have to be that way. The budgeting process is actually pretty simple in theory. The good news is, it's simple in practice too.

Before we do anything else, let's get ourselves in the right frame of mind. Sometimes it seems like we defeat ourselves before we even start. Having the right attitude makes all the difference in the world when doing a successful budget.

For many people, the word "budget" has a negative feeling to it. Some people relate it to a restrictive thing that doesn't let them breathe. Others use it as a control mechanism over their families. The truth is, it shouldn't be either of these things. All too often we associate negativity with budgets and that's a bad thing. So let's do this: If the idea of doing a budget sends you into a downward spiral of negativity, let's call it something else. How about a "spending plan" or a "cash flow plan"? Don't those sound better than budget? Call it whatever you want, as long as it puts you in the right frame of mind to get this done!

Using a Budgeting Template

When you're getting started, it may be helpful to use a premade budget sheet or template. There are many budget forms and templates out there that you can use. We personally use a free budget form (http://financialexcellence.net/wp-content/uploads/2009/12/Cash-Flow-Planning-Sheet.pdf) to manage our finances but you should use what makes sense to you and doesn't scare you away. In fact, you may not even want to use a template at all. There have been times when a yellow pad has worked just fine for me, providing I remembered all my expense categories.

Determine Your Income

How much money do you have to work with? It's hard to tell your money how to work for you if you don't even know how much you have in the first place. That's why I like to start by writing down my income. Include all income sources. I also like to work with my take home pay, not the gross pay. That lets me work with and plan for what I'll actually see in my bank account. I also like to work specifically with one month at a time and focus on the income that will hit my account in the particular month that I'm budgeting for.

Spend Money on Paper

Once you identify how much money you'll have coming into your bank account in the coming month, you can start planning what to do with that income. Start writing down your expenses on paper so you can get them in front of you in black and white. It may be easiest to work with the regular expenses you have, like rent/mortgage, insurance, taxes, phone or cable bill, etc. Next, write down your monthly irregular expenses. These are things that happen every month but are different amounts each month, like your utilities.

Now is a good time to identify all the ankle-biter expenses that sneak up on you every year. Do you give gifts for Christmas? Do you license your vehicle(s) at the same time every year? Do you have insurance bills that come every six months? Identify those expenses and plan to set aside some money each month for them so they don't destroy your budget when it's time to pay for them.

Finally, write down any exceptions to the norm. What is happening this month that doesn't happen in normal months? If you don't include those expenses in your plan, the budget won't balance. Don't forget to include savings, investments, and extra money for debt repayment in the list of expenses. These are an important part of the budget, and too many people ignore these categories until it's too late.

Balance the Budget

Now that you have your income and expenses identified and written down, it's time to balance the budget. The goal is to have your income and your expenses even out. If those two numbers are equal for the month, you have a good cash flow plan, otherwise known as a balanced budget.

In other words, when you add up your total expenses for the month and subtract them from your income, you want the difference to be zero. That means you've accounted for every dollar of your income and give each dollar a purpose within your plan.

If your expenses are higher than your income, that can be a pretty scary situation. Don't let panic set in. Take a moment to relax and calm down, then go back through the budget to find places where you can reduce your expenses. This is a hard step but it can also be very liberating to take control of your spending habits.

If your income is higher than your expenses, that means you'll have money left over (as long as you stick to the budget) at the end of the month. Before that money burns a hole in your pocket, make sure you go back into the budget and find a place to put that money. Put it in savings, pay off some debt, or whatever you want. Just make sure you have a plan for that extra money so it doesn't disappear!

But How Much Should I Budget For?

When working with people on their first budget, I often see them get overwhelmed with determining how much to budget for each category. They've never tracked their spending and they have no idea how much they typically spend on things like groceries, restaurants, or gasoline. They don't have an idea how much is an appropriate amount either. In many cases, this can cause a sort of paralysis that keeps them from moving forward. As a result, the budget never gets done at all and they give up.

If this is you, you're not alone. Don't be embarrassed. Don't be intimidated. It's not that bad.

To get an idea of how much to budget for, you can look at your bank statements for previous months. Try to identify the main categories and break your transactions into those budget categories. If that doesn't help, you can keep your receipts for a month and see where your money is going. That will give you a good idea of how much to plan for each spending category.

The Iterative Budget Process

If all else fails, just give it your best guess. That's right. Just guess. I hate to tell you this up front, but your budget is going to fail in the first month. Yep, it will FAIL. Nobody is so good that they're going to predict exactly how much gasoline or electricity they're going to consume next month. So the budget isn't going to be exactly right.

But that's a good thing. The budgeting process is iterative in nature. Your first one doesn't have to be perfect. It just has to be written out and attempted. The fun part comes when you add up all your receipts for the month and see how you did. You're going to mess up. Some categories will be overspent. Some will be under spent. And some you might actually get just right.

Now here's the trick: Don't let your mistakes get to you and become an excuse to quit. You didn't learn to ride your bike without falling off a few times. This is no different. Identify where your budget was wrong and make changes for the next month. You'll make mistakes in the next month's budget too, but not as many. Learn from those mistakes and get a little better for the following month.

After three or four months of working your budget, you'll begin to dial in your expenses and have a pretty good idea of how much to budget for each category. Maintain this progress and the mindset of continuously improving, and you'll be a budget superstar before you know it!

Matt Wegner: Matt is a Certified Financial Counselor and founder of the Financial Excellence blog at http://www.financialexcellence.net, where he shares tools and techniques for living a debt-free lifestyle.

CHAPTER 23

~~~~~~~~~~~~

Single Parenthood....

AWESOME EXPERT ADVICE

by Dorethia Conner

Guest Author & Expert Dorethia Conner Shares Financial Wisdom:

I was watching a cute YouTube video made in Britain, with quotes from other single moms and dads about their experiences in raising kids alone. It made me think of my life raising my girls, now 16 and 22. How I so desperately didn't want them to lack anything because they lived in a single-parent household and worked very hard to that end. I wondered what quote would best sum up my own experience. I began to think about how my life was in turmoil at times emotionally and financially. I recalled the many tear filled nights, wondering where on earth the money would come from for this or that. But there were also many joys. The family barbeques, school plays, adorable "wisdoms" that come from the mouth of babes and the random hug from normally reluctant teenagers. I believe my quote would be "It is worth it all!"

The joys of single parenthood are even sweeter if you have an action plan for financial stability. That's exactly what I'd like to share with you; things I learned along the way that helped me accelerate reaching the financial goals I set for my family.

So just sit back, imagine we're at your kitchen table drinking lemonade, while laughing about kids and life. Enjoy...

Education = More Income

The key challenge in single parenthood is money, plain and simple. There's only one income but the same amount of financial responsibility, multiply that by 2, 4, 6, or more kids and you really feel the pressure. Whether you have help from extended family or your children's mom or dad, you have to operate as if you are all your children have. The only adult you're in control of is yourself. You have to treat any outside help as a bonus; that includes child support.

That said, you have to increase your income and education is one key way to do so. Now don't roll your eyes at me. I'm not speaking of only the 4-year college route, that's just one option:

Two Year/Four Year Degree

1. **Trade School**

2. **Educate yourself on a serious, viable way to earn extra money such as blogging, or home cleaning, etc.**

Don't just go to school for the sake of it. Ask yourself if the degree or trade school certification is going to result in a job when you finish. Have you talked to someone who is working in your field of interest or choice?

Before my sister became a nurse she became a Certified Nursing Assistant (CNA). It was a certification she could finish pretty quickly, which also meant she would be earning more money quickly. She researched the time it would take to finish the classes and she spoke with other CNA's to learn how much money she could make and where she should apply for work once finished.

Since it was (and still is) a skill in high demand, she had no trouble finding a job and getting the salary she desired. She was able to make a very good living and take care of her children.

Learn More about Money Management

As a single parent, we have to watch every dollar. That's hard to do when you have no idea what is coming or going. You will have to become the financial expert in your home. How? Glad you asked!

1. **Read** everything you can about personal finance. Learn strategies for saving, getting out of debt, cutting cost on groceries, etc. Now, all the advice won't fit you, but you will quickly learn what works for your family. There are many websites, of course visit my blog at http://www.themoneychat.com, but in addition to Yahoo and AOL finance sites, here are a few of my favorites:

   - http://www.wisebread.com – I've been following them forever!

   - http://www.fool.com

   Great sites for single parenting tips:

   - http://www.singledadlife.com

   - http://www.singlemamanyc.com

   - http://www.pepperrific.com

2. **Write it down.** You need to budget each pay period — keep it simple: (money in) minus (money out) = balance left over

   In addition to including your basic necessities, such as housing, utilities, and transportation, include all the kid's clothes, activities, doctor visits, haircuts etc. Every dollar you expect to spend should be in your budget. Don't forget to include fun activities like going to the movies, etc.

3. **Stay away from debt.** Now, I know firsthand how one need can affect a million more. If you don't have a reliable car and there's no public transportation, you can't get to work, daycare, school, etc. So you may decide to finance a car. If you don't borrow for school you can't go, hence you can't increase your income. I get it. What I don't get is a.) not first looking for an alternative way to pay cash and b.) reckless borrowing with no payoff plan. That means a loan for a $6,000 car instead of $16,000.

4. As a single parent it's also easy to fall into credit card or payday loan debt traps. You need new furniture, you want to update the house or you are simply in the red every month. Remember that no financial "emergency" is ever the end of the world. You will pay much more in the long run, not only financially, but also emotionally, for using credit cards or payday loans. Stay away.

Finally, stick to your plan. Don't get discouraged when the best laid plans fail. It's okay, that's going to happen, just make sure you are equipped with the money smarts to get back on track. You can do it! While I'm definitely not here to sugarcoat the challenges, I will tell you that it is worth it all!

Dorethia R. Conner: Founder of #MoneyChat Blog (http://www.themoneychat.com) and online Twitter Talk Show (@MoneyChatLiVE). She is also president of Conner Financial Coaching, LLC, providing results-oriented personal finance and business coaching services. Often called upon by national media as an expert financial resource, Dorethia is passionate about helping everyday people manage their money successfully!

CHAPTER 24

~~~~~~~~

How to Gain More Time

AWESOME EXPERT ADVICE

by Jen McDonough

Time Management

People looking to earn more time and extra income will benefit from using time management skills.

What are the keys to using our allotted 168 hours per week to the fullest?

Planning and intentional living are the answers. Much like our financial budget, our time can be budgeted in the same way.

Successful time management skills can be enhanced by:

- **Identifying goals.**

- **Identifying priorities.**

- **Focusing on solutions instead of excuses.**

Looking at what we can do with our 168 hours versus what we can't do will lead to more opportunities for generating extra income.

In my book *Living Beyond Awesome*, I talk about learning how to become intentional with time and resources while training for an Ironman Triathlon. My priorities were to be a great mom and wife first while maintaining a full-time career and a household. My primary goal was to complete Ironman. Here is an example of what my training week looked like:

- *20 hours training*

- *5 hours of travel, prep time (getting equipment ready, etc.) and wrap up time (showered, dressed, etc.)*

- *40 hours at work*

- *12 hours of commute time*

- *49 hours of sleep (7 hours a night)*

- *10 hours of movies with the family (No TV shows allowed)*

- *2 hours for church*

This left me with about 30 hours if everything went as planned to spend with my family, get our grocery shopping done, do some general house chores, etc. This sounds like a lot of time to spare, but really, it wasn't. It takes serious discipline not to whittle these valuable hours away on useless things that added no value to my priorities and goals. TV was a prime example of what I stayed away from....it's basically one of those mindless (non)activities that only serves to rob us of productive time.

Tips For Gaining Time:

- **Tracking** — Track your time to see where you are spending it. Be honest in your tracking — are there things you can cut out? Are the activities you are filling your time with matching up with your goals and priorities? Give yourself permission to drop the items off that don't fall on your priority list. Focused effort leads to intentional living.

- **Schedule** — List your schedule out. If you need more time...budget it out much like you do with your money. Don't like your schedule? Be intentional and change it.

- **Task Lists** — List out your daily tasks. You can gain up to two hours worth of productivity each day when you use daily task lists. Where can you keep your list so you will actually use it each day?

- **Priorities** — List your priorities in life out. What comes first, second, and third?

- **Goals** — List your goals out using the SMARTIE method referenced in chapter 26. Be sure these goals fit into what your top priorities are.

- **Prioritization** — Life is not linear. Continuously prioritizing our priorities and goals to match our use of time is essential to successful time management.

Remember…it isn't JUST 168 hours per week to waste; you HAVE a gift of 168 hours a week to use wisely.

Live Beyond Awesome!

Jen

CHAPTER 25

Help! I have a Reluctant Spouse
AWESOME EXPERT ADVICE
by Jen McDonough

How the heck does one get their reluctant spouse on board with this finance stuff?

Being that money issues are the number one cause for divorce today, it is not surprising that having a reluctant spouse is common. This is due to many reasons including:

- What our beliefs are.
- How our parents handled finances.
- The circumstances under which we were raised.
- What our personality types are.
- What experiences we encounter as adults.

Regardless of the reasons why, it is frustrating for both parties when we are sitting on opposite sides of the money fence.

So what are some ways to get a reluctant spouse on board?

First, we need to understand and respect that everyone handles and processes things differently. Once we acknowledge this fact, we can find solutions. Some solutions that may help for your family include:

1. **Learning Style** — Understand how your spouse processes information. Are they a visual, auditory, or a kinesthetic learner? Would your spouse more likely read a book, watch a video, or just wing it and learn as they go?

2. **Personality Style** — What are your personality styles? An extrovert might enjoy financial classes that are offered in groups. An introvert may prefer to either read a book or watch a video online. Investing a few minutes and dollars into personality profiles such as the DISC profile (information can be found on our website) is well worth it.

3. **Outside Influences** — Is your spouse influenced by others around them? Whose opinions do they value? Find those people and tap into them for assistance. Ideas include mentors, friends, councilors, coaches, pastoral staff, colleagues, and relatives.

4. **Communication** — How are you presenting this information to your spouse? Are you nagging or encouraging them about finances? Are they only hearing what is being taken away from them or are you talking about goals and dreams? Are you quoting others as being experts and are they are seeing that as being a threat and/or disrespectful? How can you help improve communication? Some ideas include:

   • **Dreams/Goals** — Talk about the reasons why you want to change your finances. Listen to your spouse's dreams and what they would want to do if your family was financially free. Stop talking about what is only being taken away and focus rather on what lay ahead. See the **Sample Debt Elimination Inspiration Chart** at the end of this chapter as an example of what you could have with making sacrifices today in order to have incredible rewards tomorrow.

- **Include** — Involve your spouse, don't run them over. Remember, it is always easier to walk with someone rather than to push or pull them along.

- **Compromise** — Compromise when needed on the small things in order to get to the big things that are important. For example, if you are disagreeing on the amount on budgeted grocery expenses, as long as your budget isn't going over and you are making progress to your goal, take a chill pill and ease up. If it slows up your progress a bit, that is okay. Much better to arrive at the finish line together versus either not arriving at all or arriving separately.

5. **Trust and Actions** — Are your past actions affecting your spouse's trust level? Do you have a history of not following through on things, rushing into dead end quick rich schemes, etc? If so, what action steps can you take to earn your spouse's trust? Ideas include:

- **Progress** — Set goals together and follow up on them regularly. Where are you at with your short-term goals (i.e. are you tracking your expenses each day, logging expenses, staying within budget, etc.) and your long-term goals (i.e. how much debt has been eliminated, how much to go before that dream vacation or whatever your goals and dreams are, etc.)?

- **Meet Regularly** — Turning off the TV for 30 minutes each week to speak face to face with NO interruptions will help not only your finances, but also help strengthen your marriage.

- **Be Consistent** — Stay focused and remain consistent on your promises and actions. If you struggle in remaining consistent, revisit my article (visit chapter 26) on setting and achieving goals.

- **Tools** — Is your family equipped with the appropriate tools, support, and resources? If not, talk about solutions on how to find valuable tools, support, and resources (see our website for ideas).

Lastly, realize that debt may only be the symptom to a much deeper problem such as communication issues. If this is the case, consider seeking out professional guidance for help. Suggestions on where to find help include:

- **Church**

- **EAP (Employee Assistance Program) through employers**

- **Councilors**

- **Trusted advisors**

- **Coaches**

I would love to hear your questions, suggestions and/or success stories. Drop me a line through my website at http://www.TheIronJen.com.

Best of luck!

Jen

Sample Debt Elimination Inspiration Chart:

Client 1 - Implementation

Opens tax-deferred account at 12% and invests $2,000 each year for six years, then stops investing.*

Age	Payment	Accumulation End of Year	Age	Payment	Accumulation End of Year
22	$2,000	$2,400	45	0	$139,788
23	2,000	4,479	46	0	156,563
24	2,000	7,559	47	0	175,351
25	2,000	10,706	48	0	196,393
26	2,000	14,230	49	0	219,960
27	2,000	18,178	50	0	246,355
28	0	20,359	51	0	275,917
29	0	22,803	52	0	309,028
30	0	25,539	53	0	346,111
31	0	28,603	54	0	387,644
32	0	32,036	55	0	434,161
33	0	35,880	56	0	486,261
34	0	40,486	57	0	544,612
35	0	45,008	58	0	609,966
36	0	50,409	59	0	683,162
37	0	56,458	60	0	765,141
38	0	63,233	61	0	856,958
39	0	70,821	62	0	959,793
40	0	79,320	Total Contribution		$12,000
41	0	88,838			
42	0	99,499			
43	0	111,439	Total Accumulation		$959,793
44	0	124,811			

Client 2 - Procrastination

Spends $2,000 per year on himself for six years then opens tax-deferred account at 12% and invests $2,000 each year for 30 years.*

Age	Payment	Accumulation End of Year	Age	Payment	Accumulation End of Year
22	$0	0	45	$2,000	$124,379
23	0	0	46	2,000	142,105
24	0	0	47	2,000	161,397
25	0	0	48	2,000	183,005
26	0	0	49	2,000	207,206
27	0	0	50	2,000	234,310
28	2,000	2,240	51	2,000	264,668
29	2,000	4,749	52	2,000	298,688
30	2,000	7,559	53	2,000	336,748
31	2,000	10,706	54	2,000	379,398
32	2,000	14,230	55	2,000	427,166
33	2,000	18,178	56	2,000	480,665
34	2,000	22,559	57	2,000	540,585
35	2,000	27,551	58	2,000	607,695
36	2,000	33,097	59	2,000	682,859
37	2,000	39,309	60	2,000	767,042
38	2,000	46,266	61	2,000	861,327
39	2,000	54,058	62	2,000	966,926
40	2,000	62,785	Total Contribution		$70,000
41	2,000	72,559			
42	2,000	83,507			
43	2,000	95,767	Total Accumulation		$966,926
44	2,000	109,499			

CHAPTER 26

≈≈≈≈≈≈≈

Goal-Setting Tips

AWESOME EXPERT ADVICE

by Jen McDonough

Goals just rock! They are the destination to our finish line. We can set our sights on a goal then aim for it.

What are some awesome goal techniques I have picked up over the years?

Using goals in what I call my SMARTIE method has been incredibly helpful.

Jen's SMARTIE Goal Tips:

S: Specific! Successful goals are specific written goals.

M: Measurable! Goals require measurable outcomes with timelines along with milestones along the way to mark your progress.

A: Action! Goals require action!

R: Reach! Set goals that require you to stretch and reach out of your comfort zone.

T: Track! Track your progress consistently and review your progress regularly.

I: Incremental! Long-term goals that are worth accomplishing will be conquered in incremental steps over time, NOT overnight.

E: Enjoy! Make sure as you hit your milestones that you take time to celebrate and enjoy!

Along with SMARTIE goals, what are some great tips?

- Write your specific goals down no matter how impossible they seem and keep them in a visible place where you can see them daily.

- List your priorities out and be sure to work your goals AROUND your priorities.

- Make a list each week of the 2-3 things you want to accomplish each day/week to hit your short-term goals that lead to your long-term goals.

- Visualize accomplishing your overall goals and say them out loud regularly.

- Focus on 1-3 goals at a time versus trying to do too many.

- Share them with your trusted advisors and keep them from the Negative Nellies in your life.

- Keep in mind that victory is won with intentional incremental steps toward your goal.

A great example of one of my real goals I used in completing Ironman included:

- Complete Ironman Triathlon on November 1st in less than 14 hours.

    * Finish the 2.4 mile swim in less than 2 hours and 20 minutes without drowning.

        ◊ Take 6 Total Immersion swimming lessons to learn how to swim by February 1st.

Along with my main goal, you can see I broke my swim portion of the event into smaller incremental goals. After each incremental goal was accomplished, I took time to look back and enjoy.

Let goals become your launch pad to success!

Live Beyond Awesome!

Jen

CHAPTER 27

Awesome Personal Living Beyond
Rich Contract

AWESOME PERSONAL LIVING BEYOND RICH CONTRACT

If you want to change your financial situation, I encourage you to start by saying out loud:

"I believe in myself! Today is my day! Today I start my freedom finance journey!"

Why not take it a step further and write it down?

"I will commit to investing in myself in order to live an awesome life filled with empowerment and peace. By believing in myself, I know I will succeed on my freedom finance journey in order to

Live a Life of Awesomeness™."

An awesome financial life to me would look like:

_____

_____

_____

_____

_____

_____

_____

_____

_____

When I look back, I want to remember why I started my freedom finance journey. I started because:

_____

_____

_____

_____

_____

_____

_____

_____

_____

_____

My goals for the next month include:

1.

2.

3.

My goals for the year include:

1.

2.

3.

My goals for next 5 years include:

1.

2.

3.

When I hit low points in my journey, resources I will turn to as my sources of encouragement will include:

1.

2.

3.

The mentors, accountability partners, friends, etc. I commit to intentionally meet with on a regular basis to help me on my journey include:

1.

2.

3.

My name is: _____

and on this date: _____

I took my first steps to gaining freedom, peace, and empowerment in my life.

Congratulations on taking your first steps to Living Beyond Rich™!

PART VI
Awesome Resources

CHAPTER 28

～～～～～

3 Tips to Help Build in Positive Influences Into Your Day

Sprinkle On Some Awesome Sauce!

Having resources that you can turn to on days when you feel tired will keep you from tossing in the towel and help guide you to take another step closer to achieving your goal(s). Here are three tips to help build in positive influences into your day:

1. Materials — Have your positive influence materials ready at all times.

    *   Download your podcasts in advance to use while exercising, driving in the car, or just out and about.

    *   Keep a bag in your car packed with reading materials. This will ensure you are prepared to read during wasted downtimes such as in the doctor's office, waiting for your car repair, waiting to pick someone up, etc.

2. Journal — Have something to journal with on you at all times (I have used a few things, but lately I have enjoyed using Evernote app on my phone – paper works just fine too). Journaling can be incredibly helpful to see where you are going and where you have come from. It can also be therapeutic to write your thoughts out.

3. People — Prepare ahead of time a list of friends, mentors, and/or coaches for times when you need positive influences to speak into your life.

CHAPTER 29

~~~~~~~~

Budget Tool Suggestions

Sprinkle On Some Awesome Sauce!

Whatever budgeting tool you decide on, pick one that you will USE. Using a budgeting tool is essential to your financial success. Here are some suggestions:

- Notepad

- Excel

- Crown Financial (http://crownfinancial.org) — Plenty of free resources for budgets

- YNAB (You Need A Budget (http://www.YNAB.com) — Paid template download that is very popular.

- My Total Money Makeover (http://mytotalmoney-makeover.com) — Dave Ramsey's paid subscription program (this is what we used during our journey).

CHAPTER 30

~~~~~~~~~~

We Need "I Believe In You" Type Influences In Our Life

Sprinkle On Some Awesome Sauce!

Who we choose to surround ourselves will be who we become. Seek out positive people who will build you up rather than tear you down. We all need to hear "I believe in you" during periods in our life. Here are three suggestions on where to look for some of your "I believe in you" people:

1. Consider finding an accountability partner where you can meet in person, virtually (i.e. Skype), and/or through email on a regular basis.

2. Look for positive outside influences to speak into your life such as a coach, a pastor, a councilor, etc.

3. Consider joining or starting your own Mastermind group (see http://www.48day.com for information on how to start one). This is a great way to connect with people seeking similar things in life as you are.

IMPORTANT: Stay away from the negative people and media sources as they will only take you down. Like the old saying goes, one can't fly with the eagles if they are hanging out with the turkeys.

CHAPTER 31

~~~

Having the Right Attitudes
Are Empowering

Sprinkle On Some Awesome Sauce!

Positive attitudes will play a large part in your financial success.

There will be periods in your life where you will want to dip into the "Scarlett O'Hara poor me" attitude when life smacks you in the face. This is common, especially when you are going through financial troubles.

The key is to recognize we all have a choice on how we want our attitude to be at all times. There are some people who will choose to live in a "poor me" type of mentality for the rest of their life. Someone or something is always preventing them from being joyful. These people will always remain poor.

You are not one of those people. How can I tell? You made it this far in the book which tells me you are determined to win.

Here are three tips to get your attitude back on track when you hit hard times:

- For every one complaint you have, name three things you are grateful for.

- Quit the sighing and smile even when you don't feel like it.

- Volunteer your time to help out where people are less fortunate.

Remember, taking action to having a positive attitude is possible. No matter what outside influences happen, it really is possible for everyone to live beyond awesome.

CHAPTER 32

≈≈≈≈≈≈≈

Finding Your Passion in Work is Possible

Sprinkle On Some Awesome Sauce!

Earning money by doing what you love IS possible.

Over half of our population today dislikes their jobs and would change if they could. Wouldn't it be nice to earn more money, work less hours, and do what you love to do? Sound enticing?

Here are four books I recommend for discovering your passion and learning how to transition to the work you love:

1. *No More Dreaded Mondays* by **Dan Miller**

2. *When Wisdom Meets Passion* by **Dan Miller**

3. *Passions ebook* by **Joel and Pei Boggess**

4. *Quitter* by **Jon Acuff**

Remember, it is possible to find passion in the work you do. It just takes intentional ACTION towards making it happen.

CHAPTER 33

~~~~~~~~

3 Ways to Improve Chances
of Landing a Job

Sprinkle On Some Awesome Sauce!

When one is losing or has lost a job, it is easy to get caught up in panic, worry, and self-doubt. Who could blame a person as there is so much gloom and doom around us.

When looking for a job, remember your emotional state is transparent during job interviews. People are not just looking for the right answers; they are looking for the right person. Body language and how you present yourself are just as important as what you say if not more important.

So what is a person to do when they find themselves in a fearful predicament of needing to find a job?

Here are three easy ways to help convey you are the right person for the job:

I. Be Positive — Consciously stop whining and complaining thoughts from whirling around in your head. Use intentional language to promote positive transformational outcomes (PTO) for yourself. Phrases such as:

- "I will" (instead of "I should")

- "I can" (instead of "I wish")

- "I have" (instead of "if only I had")

2. Be Confident — Keep your body language in check. Smile, pull your shoulders back, and walk fast. When you do this, it makes it difficult for one to be down in the dumps. Act confident and you will become confident. Remember, someone/someplace is going to be lucky to have you working for them!

3. Take Care of Yourself — Be intentional in keeping your emotional energy tank full. Examples include:

- Exercise

- Meditate

- Make time with friends & family, hobbies, etc.

When you keep your emotional tank full, you will be able to keep your "cup overflowing" and in turn give to others while keeping yourself energized.

Being out of work is hard enough without having emotional drainers in your life. You only have a limited amount of time and resources — use them well and avoid negative influences as much as possible (reference back to Chapter 30 on where to seek positive influences).

Remember, success takes intentional action no matter what life throws at you.

CHAPTER 34

～～～～～

3 Ways to Get Your Medical Debt In Order

Sprinkle On Some Awesome Sauce!

With medical debt being the number one cause of bankruptcy today, it is not unusual for people to find themselves drowning in debt when a medical event hits their lives.

Here are some ways to help patients to get their medical debt organized:

First off, remember to Breathe! — Having medical events happen in your life can be stressful enough. Toss on all the extra financial burdens and you are looking at not only additional stress, but also additional health problems stemming off of all this stress. Relax and know that with intentional living, you WILL have your life back in order when you take intentional steps to find solutions. Next steps include:

1. HOW TO HANDLE BILLS — Gather up all your medical related statements including the Explanation of Benefit (EOB) forms sent from your insurance company as well as your medical bills and put them in ONE place. Go through them and:

2. Keep ONLY the current bill for each provider. Toss out any redundant old copies.

- Match up EACH Explanation of Benefit statement (EOB) to each medical bill.

- Highlight the PATIENT RESPONSIBILITY portion on each EOB and ensure that corresponds with your medical bill. Ensure that your medical bill and EOB match up. If they don't contact your insurance company for assistance.

- List each medical debt into your debt snowball and list it from smallest to largest.

- IMPORTANT: BE PROACTIVE AND CONTACT YOUR MEDICAL PROVIDER'S BILLING OFFICE DIRECTLY TO SET UP A PAYMENT PLAN (DO NOT WAIT FOR THEM TO CONTACT YOU).

  I. By contacting the billing office directly, you are showing yourself to be a person who is taking intentional steps in paying your bill which they appreciate.

  II. Ask to be set up on a regular monthly payment plan that will fit into your budget.

  III. If you are unable to set up a payment plan within your budget, do NOT over promise what you can't afford. Instead, ask to speak to the head of the organization. If that doesn't work, continue to send what regular payments you can afford.

    - Hospitals and clinics are usually willing to work with you on a payment plan. If you are unable to get help, let them know you will be transferring care.

    - NOTE: If you know you will have large amounts of out of pocket expenses ahead of time, be proactive in working with their billing department ahead of time. Some places will offer upfront discounts for patients who are paying out of pocket.

3. HOW TO HANDLE LARGE OUT OF POCKET EXPENSES — If you have an extraordinarily large amount of out of pocket expenses that are going to take you years to pay off, consider the following:

- Contact the medical administrator leader for the healthcare provider that is billing you (preferably in person, however, if not an option, at least by phone and/or letter).

  I. Express gratitude for the care you have received and explain your goal is to pay every penny back.

  II. Have your written budget ready to reference — this will help answer any questions and show that you are being intentional in paying off your debt.

  III. Ask if they would be willing to write off some of the medical expenses and set you up on monthly payment plan that fits into your budget.

  IV. Depending on your situation, consider requesting a deeper discount if you are able to get a loan from your local bank or credit union to pay the debt in full and at the same time have the loan be in payments that fit your budget. DISCLAIMER: While I do NOT endorse taking out loans to incur more debt, I do find that in certain circumstances it IS okay to transfer the debt to someone else as long as you know that this doesn't give you the freedom to use that loan to spend on other things.

- If working with a hospital facility, contact them to see if they have a patient advocate/social worker type person that can provide you with additional resources.

CHAPTER 35

─〰〰〰〰─

Claim Not Blame
Problem-Solving Method

Sprinkle On Some Awesome Sauce!

Making excuses is a convenient copout for staying in a 'poor me' mentality state of life. There is ALWAYS a "but, I can't because…" type excuse waiting to be used for all us.

If you are continuously making excuses about your situation, my advice is to "STOP!"

Why is this so important?

- Ditching the constant use of excuses and instead finding solutions WILL propel you into becoming victorious.

- Continuously seeking out solutions will get you to your financial goals whereas excuses will keep you trapped in muck.

The ICAN problem-solving method is a great tool for getting you started how to continuously problem-solve. After a while, the ICAN™ problem-solving method will become second nature:

Issue: Identify the ISSUE — What is the problem? Is this problem a symptom of a much bigger problem that I need to address?

Cause: Identify the CAUSE — Why is this issue happening? How can I take personal responsibility?

Answer: Identify the ANSWER — What are possible solutions? How can I find creative out of the box solutions versus just looking at the obvious?

NO Excuses: Simply put, NO EXCUSES — How can I stop myself from making excuses? What action steps can I take instead?

Two awesome books I recommend on learning the power of taking personal responsibility are:

QBQ! The Question Behind the Question by John G. Miller

Flipping the Switch: Unleash the Power of Personal Accountability Using the QBQ! by John G. Miller

CHAPTER 36

Taking Action is Key

Sprinkle On Some Awesome Sauce!

It is one thing to dream of becoming rich, but it is quite another to take action to become rich.

My best advice to you on taking action to achieve financial success is:

- "MOVE IT." Don't wait for perfection, just start now.

- Learn from the best and then put this education to use in your own life.

- Forgive and keep moving when you goof up.

Becoming debt free and living an abundant life is possible. However, if you are sitting around waiting to become rich, it isn't going to happen. Intentional action is required.

Here are three steps to take in getting your finances in order:

- Put a stake in the ground and take action to put together a budget.

- Say enough is enough and take action each day to live on a written budget.

- Take action to get back on your budget no matter how many times you goof up.

Three things to keep in mind as you take action to change your finances:

- Remember, no one is born knowing this stuff, so be patient with yourself.

- You are never going to have a perfect month, so get over it.

- You are going to do AWESOME when you take action. REMEMBER: the key to achieving 'awesomeness' starts with remember your ABC's (Action Brings Change).

CHAPTER 37

~~~~~~~~~~

How to Gain Positive Transformational Outcomes (PTO)

Sprinkle On Some Awesome Sauce!

Want positive transformational outcomes (PTO) in your own life?

PTO becomes possible when we intentionally take action to live a more meaningful and purposeful life.

How can you do this?

Look for ways to reaffirm how you will live your life. What are you reading? What are you allowing yourself to listen to? Who are you hanging out with?

The language we use is incredibly powerful in shaping the way we live. Both in terms of how we speak to ourselves and how we speak to others.

PTO can be created by intentionally saying out loud how you will live your life. Consider saying the following out loud weekly and see what happens:

I WILL Live With HOPE!

I WILL Live With Conviction – BELIEVE!

I WILL Live With INTENTION!

I WILL Live With COURAGE!

I WILL Live With FAITH!

I WILL Live With PASSION!

I WILL Live With MOTIVATION!

I WILL Live With PERSEVERANCE!

I WILL Live With PURPOSE!

I WILL Live With INTEGRITY!

I WILL Live With RESILIENCE!

I WILL Live With GENEROSITY!

I WILL Live With CONTENTMENT!

I WILL Live With GRATITUDE!

What are some "I will" type of statements you can add to your own list? REMEMBER: Success happens when we begin with our ABC's (Action Brings Change).

CHAPTER 38

Resource Links

Much of the resources below can be found on my website at:
http://www.TheIronJen.com

AWESOME RESOURCES REFERENCED

Dan Miller:

http://www.48days.com

http://www.48days.net

Dave Ramsey

http://www.daveramsey.com

AWESOME BUDGET RESOURCES

http://www.YNAB.com

http://mytotalmoneymakeover.com

http://crownfinancial.org

AWESOME EXPERTS

Ashley Barnett: http://moneytalkscoaching.com/

Dorethia R. Conner: http://www.themoneychat.com

- http://www.wisebread.com

- http://www.fool.com

- http://www.singledadlife.com

- http://www.singlemamanyc.com

- http://www.pepperrific.com

Jennifer Finnegan: http://www.singlemomm.org/

Jeff Pattison: http://www.jeffpattison.com

Glen Steinson: http://www.StewardshipWeekly.com

Steve Stewart: http://www.moneyplansos.com/

Jackie Walters: http://thebudgetworks.com

Matt Wegner: http://www.financialexcellence.net

http://financialexcellence.net/wp-content/uploads/2009/12/Cash-Flow-Planning-Sheet.pdf

YOUR AWESOME NOTES

YOUR AWESOME NOTES

YOUR AWESOME NOTES

YOUR AWESOME NOTES

YOUR AWESOME NOTES

YOUR AWESOME NOTES

YOUR AWESOME NOTES

YOUR AWESOME NOTES

YOUR AWESOME NOTES

Acknowledgements

Dave Ramsey & Team — THANK YOU for teaching our family how get control over our finances AND our life! You made the impossible possible as you gave us hope, inspiration, and the knowledge to take action. Our family tree has been changed... thank you for doing what you do each day!

TTMO Forums — You guys rock! Thank you for the advice and inspiration over the years.

Dan Miller — Thank you for giving me the belief and knowledge that we ALL have the ability to do great things when find our passion in the work we love to do. Thank you for blessing our family with your continuous messages of inspiration, hope and wisdom. I am living out my passion today because of your ministry...thank you!

48Days.Net — This group knocks it out of the park! Thank you for being a source of encouragement, motivation, and information. Synergy is awesome and this group proves it!

My Awesome Editors — To the group of people who have helped me create the vision to see this through...thank you!!! Your abilities and talents amaze me. Thank you for your honesty, your feedback, and your wisdom! Thank you Mark Anderson, Pei Boggess, Bill Conlan, Dan Conlan, Kathleen Crandall, Trish Englund, Bill Fredericks, Lori Garrick, Teresa Munson, and Nyasha Kanganga for sharing your wisdom, time, and talents into making a lump of coal into a diamond!

Special Editing Thank You — Trish Englund, Dan Conlan, and Bill Conlan...I am humbled by your incredible gifts and hours you shared in order to make this project a success. Thank you!

My Awesome Expert Contributors — I am blessed to have had each of you contribute awesome material that is going to reach people. I admire each of you for the ministries you providing in educating and reaching every day people to discover freedom and peace. Thank you Ashley Barnett, Dorethia Conner, Kathleen Crandall, Jennifer Finnegan, Jeff Pattison, Glen Steinson, Steve Stewart, Jackie Walters, and Matt Wegner for being a part of this project!!

Uma Valeti & Family — Wow, talk about being a great mentor on paying it forward in life. You guys ROCK! Thank you for your amazing gifts of generosity, kindness, and "wonderfulness!"

Kathleen Crandall — You are one of the MANY blessings we have encountered on this journey...I can't thank you enough for all you have done my friend! I can't wait for your book!

Jane Mueller — Your friendship and love has been an incredible gift, blessing, and joy over the past 33 years! Thank you for always being there pal!

Mom — Thank you for your continued love and support. Sorry it took us a few years to catch on to this finance stuff... guess what though? We finally got it!

To my AWESOME kids (Maggie, Robbie, Max, and Remy) — Both your dad and I are so proud of each of you! We are the luckiest parents in the world and believe in each of you. Remember to continue to let God lead your hearts and continue to follow your passions throughout your lifetime. Teach your kids to the same and I promise you that you will not regret it.

Maggie McDonough — I believe you will do great things Maggie. You have the charisma and personality to make great things happen in life. We are so proud of your joyful and generous heart— you continue to inspire us to be generous. Thank you Nanny. I love you!

Robbie McDonough — I believe you will do great things Robbie. You have a knack for being adventurous to make great things happen. We are so proud of your ability willingness to teach and educate others — we continue to learn from you. Thank you Robbie Dunna. I love you!

Max McDonough — I believe you will do great things Max. Your joyful and spontaneous personality will lead you to great things in life. We are so proud of your compassion and empathy for those in need —you inspire us to do the same. Thank you Maxidoodle. I love you!

Remy McDonough — I believe you will do great things Remy. Your determination and energy will continuously question the status quo in life. We are so proud of your sweet heart – you keep us young. Thank you Remster. I love you!

Bob McDonough — My rock, my best friend, and my favorite husband in the whole world. Thank you for patience and understanding in letting me follow my dreams. Your daily doses of encouragement, humor, and love mean the world to me. Thank you for believing in me through your words and actions. I can't think of another person that I would have wanted to go through good and bad times with. I admire your courage, strength, and wisdom. I love Living Beyond Awesome with you kiddo! Eggs, one more thing...dang we rock at this stuff don't we? Love you!

God — Thank you for every lesson and every blessing!

Connect With Jen

Jen McDonough lives in Lindstrom, Minnesota with her handsome husband, four awesome kids, two dogs, and one ugly mortgage.

She is an ordinary person living an extraordinary life. As an engaging speaker, author, and coach, she demonstrates to her audiences that taking intentional ACTION leads organizations and individuals to success.

Audiences connect with her authenticity as she shares real life stories that are filled with humor, fear, pain, embarrassment, success, faith, joy, hope, inspiration, and positive transformational outcomes (PTO's).

Jen is the accomplished author of *Living Beyond Awesome* which has peaked in Amazon's Top 100 Book Categories and Amazon's Top 100 Kindle Categories. Her latest book, *Living Beyond Rich*, has been endorsed by such people as:

- Chris LoCurto, Vice President and Speaker at Dave Ramsey's Organization

- National Bestselling Authors Dan Miller and John G. Miller

- Nationally recognized speakers and coaches such as kent Julian, Dr. Pei Boggess, Rob Clinton, and Joel Boggess

Remember, if she can do it, YOU can do it! Take action today to live an extraordinary tomorrow.

Book Jen for your next speaking event or just stop by to say hi by connecting with her at http://www.TheIronJen.com or on Twitter (@TheIronJen).